Whizz

From Zero to Hero

David Pugh and Lynn Cavendish

Copyright © 2022
Lynn Cavendish David Pugh

All rights reserved. No part of this publication maybe reproduce, stored in retrieval system or transmitted in any or by any means, electronic, mechanical, photo-copy recording or otherwise without prior written consent of the copyright owner. Nor can be circulated in any from of binding or cover other than that in which it is published and without similar condition including this condition being imposed on a subsequent publisher.

For the personal protection of persons within this publication, names in some cases have been altered and any similarities to any person's or person living or dead is totally coincidental.

The right of Lynn Cavendish and David Pugh to be identified as the author of this work has been asserted in accordance with the Copyright Designs and Patents Act 1988

Table of Contents

Dedication i
About the Author ii
Prologue iii
Chapter One: For the Love of Dogs 1
Chapter Two: Jaws of Death 10
Chapter Three: The Prince and the Pauper 26
Chapter Four: Omega Male 42
Chapter Five: Big Pawprints to Fill 53
Chapter Six: Bang, Crash, Splash! 78
Chapter Seven: Newfound Friends 97
Chapter Eight: Festivals and Heroes 117
Chapter Nine: Swansea 131
Chapter Ten: Whizz's First Rescue 146
Chapter Eleven: Topper Comes a Cropper 155
Chapter Twelve: Toni Curtis and the Cabbage Patch 176
Chapter Thirteen: Whizz and Ellie Bedford 191
Chapter Fourteen: The Bridge 214
Chapter Fifteen: Be Prepared 228
Chapter Sixteen: Whizz and Steph 250
Chapter Seventeen: The Russian Lifeguard 261
Chapter Eighteen: Oxwich Bay 284
Chapter Nineteen: The Hoff – Baywatch 300
Chapter Twenty: The Beginning of the Last Goodbye 312
Chapter Twenty-One: The Legacy 330
Epilogue 339

Dedication

This book is dedicated to the charity 'Newfound Friends'.

The charity has helped a huge number of children and adults alike. Many terminally ill children have experienced the love, affection, and companionship from David's dogs.

The charity has raised millions to help many other charities; at the time of publication, fifty-seven in all and still counting as the numbers increase each year.

About the Author

David has trained Newfoundland dogs for over thirty-six years, building on their natural ability to detect and rescue people in trouble as swimming dogs. He has owned seven Newfoundlands, but Whizz was the ultimate standout of all the dogs that David has nurtured. It is David's ambition that the world is told of this incredible dog, who was one in a million and MUST be a part of history, never to be forgotten.

Lynn Cavendish is an established, published author in her own right, having two successful fiction novels already released, each achieving five-star reviews. David approached her to co-write this book, to which she agreed with great pleasure.

Prologue

Stuck in the traffic on the M25 on my way to the Isle of Dogs London, my mind began to wonder about my faithful friend Whizz. Whizz passed away only a few weeks before he was to be honored with the OBE for services to mankind. My dog really deserved the award, and it was such a shame he could not be there to receive it. In the absence of our hero, the posthumous medal was to be placed on Whizz's cousin Tizz – his nearest and closest friend.

The traffic finally cleared as we headed to the Scouts Docklands Project Canary Wharf. It was a place Whizz knew well, as he had attended many charity days there performing many sponsored rescues. What a setting the docks were, surrounded by immense towering offices – many from the international banking community!

Whizz left a big hole in my life, and I mean BIG – a twelve-and-a-half stone wonder who leapt into my world and made a huge splash that is still ripping out even now. A great shaggy, black and white coat covered his massive form, topped with a glossy black head, sporting a blaze of white that stretched from his big wet nose to his forehead. His large floppy ears flew like a pixie when he cannoned into the water, fired by immense speckled legs tipped with huge chunky paws resting on my forearms, as he stood tall like a bear.

His eyes, though small, oozed large pools of caramel, swirling with character, strength, and spirit. Occasionally, I would look into them and try to find out where it all came from. I wish I could say it originated from myself – that I was the one that trained him and turned him into the water rescue dog that saved ten lives, but to be honest, I cannot take the credit. Whizz had a bumpy start to life; I gave him a stable home, lots of love and affection, together with the opportunity to go swimming; that's it.

No doubt he learned a lot from the other dogs we owned and met; however, Whizz had something extra… Self-confidence, intelligence, and skills harked back to the breeding heritage of working water dogs.

The first Newfoundlands, active in the icy waters off the east coast of the Canadian mainland, recovered fishing nets for the local fishermen and towed shipwrecked sailors to safety. Over the centuries, I believe some of the heroic mettle has been bred out of Newfoundlands over the years, whose reputation these days is, above all, the gentle giant. Whizz had both those attributes in bucket loads and beyond.

I am full of mixed emotions as I sit here waiting to collect the PDSA Order of merit in his name. Whizz was only the third dog to receive this award; the others were in service with the Metropolitan police. It was a very proud moment but full of sadness as Whizz could not be there himself.

Whizz was a once-in-a-lifetime dog, but no, that's not true – I could easily have gone a lifetime and never met a dog like him.

Chapter One: For the Love of Dogs

It was a cold, gloomy evening in December when I drove along the secluded lane and parked outside the old farmhouse. The building was dark and strangely eerie, displaying no evidence of life; I had a feeling they'd forgotten I was coming.

Braced against the night chill, I vacated the van, trudged the garden path, and rang the doorbell. Somewhere inside, a dog barked. That was Jake, the owner's German Shepherd. I'd met him a few times. He was handsome and a giant compared to the normal of his breed.

There was no other sign of occupation. 'Fine', I thought, sinking my cold hands into my pockets. 'I'll give it a minute.'

It was a smart modern house, built by the owner himself on the grounds of an old farmstead. He was a professional builder and my best customer, which was why I loathed walking away. In the van, I had a stack of bespoke window frames that I'd promised to drop off on the way home from my joinery business in North Bristol.

I knocked on the door, and three sharp raps set Jake off again. I pictured him at the foot of the stairs, barking his head off at the letterbox.

"S'alright boy," I murmured under my breath. "It's only me."

Still no answer. Growing impatient, I went round to the side of the house and knocked on the patio door, feeling like a sneaky burglar.

Somewhere inside, a light pinged on; I ripped back to the front. Moments later, the door flew open. In that split second, I had just enough time to see a casually dressed woman in her thirties standing on the threshold. I had met her a few times before and was about to open my mouth to give a cheery greeting, only to leave it gaping motionless, as Jake hurtled past her, lunged at me like a hungry lion, and clamped his jaws round my nether regions.

I don't think I even cried out; the pain sucked the air from my lungs. I was aware of the lady of the house shrieking, "Jake, no! Off!" and remember pushing at the dog's rippling neck, trying to wrench free, my heart pounding.

The builder's wife yanked Jake's collar, which could only have been a moment before he recognised me, then released his wolf-like grip, backing off panting. His mistress pulled the muscular hulk of the animal into the back kitchen, then shut the door on him.

"Oh my God, are you alright?" she blurted, rushing back. "Did he hurt you?"

I could feel the dampness in my trousers, blood sliding down my leg, and pooling in the cuff of my boot. "No, no," I choked out a feigned chuckle and waved her off. "I'm fine, I'm fine – no harm done."

No harm done? Hmm... I don't know how I off-loaded all those windows, hobbling back and forth to the van! I was too embarrassed to tell the builder's wife the truth; it was just not me.

By the time I was done, and back in the van, the adrenaline was wearing off, and I was nauseous with the pain. Realizing I could not go home, I gave my wife Jean a quick call, glossing over the gory details like I always did, then drove to Bristol Royal Infirmary.

'Twas the season to binge drink and fall over; thus, A&E was full of the usual festive unfortunates; one young woman was still wearing a Rudolph headband as she slouched against her bleary-eyed friend. I thought the colour of her nose set off the outfit completely.

I sat with my legs crossed, nervously checking the floor every now and then to check I wasn't leaking blood.

You cannot blame the dog – can't blame a guard dog for guarding, although I had visited the house before and got on well with Jake. He's obviously spotted that his owner was not expecting me, so I was a legitimate threat, or he mistook me for the vet and wreaked instant revenge for the tragic removal of his manly pride and joys.

I was actually very fond of dogs. My whole life has moved around canines, and extremely large ones too. During my childhood, there was always a Collie curled up under the kitchen table or a German Shepherd hurtling across the park to fetch me a stick. Then in my thirties, I discovered Newfoundlands, one of the biggest breeds on Earth.

If you have ever met one of these mighty dogs, you will understand why they have changed the course of my life. Newfies can change anyone's life if they are on a lead and choose to go in a different direction from you, which they often do! They will take over your house, flatten you against the walls as they barge past; lie across doorways, trip you up, and headbutt you as they lean in for a slobbery kiss; uh-oh, my life, they are the gentlest, most intelligent, most wonderful animals I have ever had the privilege to meet.

They are powerful swimmers, too, with a long history of saving people from drowning, which is why I run a charity showing off their water rescue skills.

"David Pugh?" I jolted out of my daze to see a young nurse scanning the sorry crowd of casualties. Gingerly, I rose to my feet and followed her out of the waiting room.

In a small treatment area, another nurse was waiting for us, skimming through some notes. She looked pale, tired, and gaunt; I was praying she would not get her mitts on me.

"I understand you have been bitten by a dog, Mr. Pugh," she said. "In the groin area?"

I gave them a brief outline of the attack, which had a whiff of slapstick comedy when you said it out loud. I could see the look on their faces, trying to be serious and professional. In fact, the ailing nurse looked even worse as she sucked in her cheeks to inwardly bite and stifle her amusement. In better times, I could have very well enjoyed a joke with two young female nurses; however, I was in too much pain to see the funny side and too little not to feel awkward.

At least it cheered up a dreary day for them both. I bet my misadventure was shared around the team that night over cigarettes and late-shift coffees – I can well imagine the comments. 'I bet he thought it was a complete balls-ache of a day' and, 'what a fuss over such a little thing!' I only hope it provided some comic relief.

The administration of the local anaesthetic was bad enough, but seeing Helga the Great standing over me, brandishing a massive needle and thread, was something else. 'Lie back and think of England' goes the phrase. I was led back but not thinking of England at all; more like I wish I had been drowned at birth. I just closed my eyes and prayed for forgiveness for all the jokes I had played on people and the bad things I had done in life.

I did not actually feel much; thus, the event was not as bad as I had anticipated. I was, however, hoping they wouldn't bandage me up completely, so I could don my trousers again. Goodness knows what Jean would have thought if I had hobbled through the door looking like I was wearing oversize incontinence pants, but the answer would have been, 'Not tonight, Josephine.'

At last, suitably stitched up, cleaned, and injected with precautionary antibiotics, I shuffled back to my van and started for home; the local was wearing off, and despite the marvellous effects of painkilling miracle drugs, I was still wincing in pain whenever I shifted in my seat.

To lift my spirits, I took the Clifton Suspension Bridge route home as there was always something inspiring about crossing this iconic Victorian landmark, twinkling with lights high above the blackness of the Avon Gorge. I was always in awe of the splendour of this engineering masterpiece; for some reason, taking a deep breath and enjoying a crossing always relieved any anxiety I felt. I'd even name one of my dogs 'Izzie' after its engineer, the great Isambard Kingdom Brunel.

As I made my way back towards my village on the edge of the city, it began to drizzle, and the windscreen wipers momentarily beat in time to the Christmas song on the radio.

I suddenly thought of my grandfather, Christopher. It dawned on me that he had actually helped to build the A&E department that had just patched me up. He, like myself, was a joiner by trade, having a well-established business in Kings Square, Bristol, and was the main contractor, working on an extension to the Bristol Royal Infirmary at the turn of the twentieth century. He is also a joiner by nature, playing for Gloucestershire Cricket Club and Bristol Rovers Football Club.

When the First World War broke out, he joined that too, signing up for the Royal Engineers with his cricket pals. He took his dog, Samuel, with him, a free-spirited mongrel, as most dogs were in those days.

On the western front, Christopher was tasked with building and shoring up tunnels, which were then packed with explosives and detonated under German lines to cause as much carnage as possible. I guess Sammy was brought along to sniff out the enemy.

One day, the tunnel my grandfather was working in collapsed, bringing a load of heavy earth down on him and two other sappers. As they lay there being crushed to death, Sammy raced back along the tunnel, barking to raise the alarm. Soldiers followed him back to the scene and managed to dig out all three men.

A few months later, my grandfather was gassed at Ypres and died from his injuries; thus, my father's father never made it home from the trenches at all. Nobody seems to know what became of brave Sammy, but in the drawer at home, along with a photograph of my grandfather, in his soldier's attire, I still have the medal Sammy was awarded by the National Canine Defence League (now called the Dog's Trust), for saving the lives of three soldiers. It was the 'doggie' Victoria cross of the day.

What a futile waste of life war is, splitting families like an axe, sending splinters into future generations.

'Never again', we say. Then again, history can repeat itself in more positive ways, which I was about to find out.

I have been told I look like my grandfather, sadly, I never met him, but I am sure if I had, we would have enjoyed a very special family bond. It is uncanny how our lives intertwined, in passions and work. As I drove home that December night, the thought of him and Sammy put my groin injury in perspective. Yes, I had been bitten in the tenderest place known to man, but other than that, I was a fit and healthy forty-six-year-old – I'd live.

In fact, when I look back on it now, that German Shepherd probably saved my life – as will become apparent as our story develops.

My Grandfather Christopher with my father William on his knee with Uncle Jim in the background. Samuel's Victoria Cross award

Chapter Two: Jaws of Death

"Drop it, Bear. Drop iiiiiiit." With a gentle tug, I freed the remote control from the jaws of our fourteen-stone Newfoundland dog and wiped the slobber off my jeans. A ritual I had carried out many times before, I am surprised my shimmering denim did not walk to the washing machine on their own; they certainly knew the way.

Aiming the magic wand at the kitchen TV, I pressed the nibbled standby button, hoping the screen would flicker into life. No such luck. "Humph... That's another one gone." Ah well, you can only have so much of Paul O'Grady, but it did keep our two giant canines amused. I am sure they looked upon their 'little' brothers with delight, digesting every bad behavior pattern in the book.

My wife Jean tutted, "He's going to end up with battery acid in his belly one of these days." Thankfully, she was grinning and gave Bear an affectionate scratch behind the ears as he laid his bulky black head in her lap.

Izzie, our other Newfoundland dog, decided to join in the fun and was licking the wall again. He had a thing about the salts in the plasterboard, and over a few weeks, he had sucked a big gaping hole into the kitchen wall above the radiator.

"Blimey!" I tutted. "We're living with a pair of vandals."

It was true. You can't be too house-proud when you live with animals, and we owned two dogs that were so large some people mistook them for bears. Occasionally, I did actually wish they were these magnificent beasts and hibernated for the winter to give us all a bit of peace.

Weighing a combined total of twenty-four stone, our hefty housemates had completely taken over our seventeenth-century cottage in North Somerset. If anyone could see the lumps they'd taken out of doors, the grit they'd dragged across floors, and the slobber they'd smeared across walls, they would have thought we'd been under attack from a pack of deranged wolves on the hunt for the two tons of dog food we keep locked in the utility room. I just hoped the cottage would still be standing in another three hundred and fifty years. In fact, I am surprised we had not sold up by now and gone to live in a cave. It would have been a whole lot easier.

It was Christmas 2003, a year after the Jake incident, and my tender regions appeared to have fully recovered. We were well into another season of goodwill. My joinery business was busy with orders, and Jean was in good spirits, despite living with chronic rheumatoid arthritis. Our daughter Colleen had just started university on the other side of the country, and our dogs were doing their best to fill the gap she had left behind.

Everything was fine. Our little (well, not so little) family was as settled and content as you possibly could be – then the phone rang. I hurried into the lounge to answer it, pursued by Izzie and Bear.

"Dave, it's Lucy here."

Lucy was a well-established Newfoundland dog breeder who I knew well, having purchased four dogs from her already.

She sounded breathless with excitement. "Have you heard about this Madam Butterfly litter?"

Well, yes, of course, I had. Newfie news travels fast, and the grapevine was bustling with excitement about a litter of three black and white puppies born in Dorset. They were the grandchildren of Madam Butterfly, a Crufts champion. Although I have no love for the dog show and its obsession with pedigree, I knew that this matriarch was an admired, if not legendary figure in Newfoundland circles.

"Would you like one?" said Lucy. "I can get you the boy if you like."

I would like to say I took this as a completely innocent offer with no strings attached, with only the puppy's interests at heart, but there was a whiff of something fishy. Dog breeding is a murky world, and I knew that in ordinary circumstances, Lucy would not be allowed anywhere near the prized bloodline of the great Madam Butterfly. These were top-notch, valuable animals, and I was suspicious.

Lucy shared her modest Devon farmhouse with her husband and accommodated up to forty Newfoundlands at a time. Clearly, she had an affinity with animals and a passion for the breed, but she confessed her chaotic household of wall-to-wall dogs was controversial.

"Run that by me again," I said, not quite trusting my ears. "You're saying I can have one of these puppies?"

"Cracker," said Lucy. "Rubbish name. Personally, I'd call him Whizz or something more friendly like that; but he's a stunning boy, really exceptional. The mother is a Russian champion and the daughter of Madam Butterfly, as I'm sure you know. You'll have to pay full price, but I can make it happen for you."

"And then what?"

"When he's old enough, you'd loan him to me as a stud dog. That's my only condition."

And there was the sting in the tail! Jean, who was now on the sofa listening to my side of the conversation, watched me shift uneasily in my armchair. Surmising the gist of the proposition, she raised her eyebrows.

Dogs are very intuitive and perfectly adept at observing body language. Izzie and Bear were no exception and, despite being serenely settled at our feet, immediately cocked their ears, jolting up. Opening their eyes wider than an insomniac owl, they gaped their salivating chops, alert to the possibility that something exciting was about to happen – a walk? A biscuit? A squeaky toy? 'Bring it on then, whatever it is!'

I winced. We had never loaned our dogs out as studs before. The wad of money It generated bore no interest, and we refused to look upon our canine friends as breeding machines – it just wasn't us.

"Are you sure you can't just come to an arrangement with the original breeder? It's Monique, isn't it?"

Lucy erupted. "She doesn't get it! She thinks I'm not good enough for a quality bloodline because I have a lot of dogs. It's rubbish. I *love* my dogs. Nobody loves Newfies more than me, but you know what it's like. It's nasty, this business; everyone bad-mouthing each other. She's obviously heard some bitchiness from another breeder and taken against me."

Hmm. I could well believe that. That's exactly why Jean and I tried to steer clear of the dog breeding world. I had heard whispers of the backstabbing that went on behind the scenes. Plus, I had my own reservations about Lucy's set-up. I knew she was competent and meant well, but how could one couple in a modest house give forty big dogs all the attention they deserved?

I was confused. "If you don't mind me asking…" I ventured. "How come Monique is prepared to sell you this puppy, then?"

"She's not," said Lucy. "I'm going through a third party."

My hackles rose; this sounded decidedly dodgy – *A third party?* I was silent for a few moments, casting my eyes around the room, taking in the holy sight of holly and tinsel above the fireplace; the nativity scene in the alcove; the cards propped up on every surface, promoting peace on Earth and goodwill to all men.

And goodwill to all animals? I felt a stab of dread, feeling that I was being drawn into something very dubious indeed. I looked down at Izzie and Bear, who had decided, nothing was going on after all and were both snoozing contently on the rug. A dog is for life, not just for Christmas; we already had two beautiful ones. Why on earth would we want another?

Izzie and Bear were both of a breed known as Landseers, being so named after the nineteenth-century artist Edward Landseer who famously painted these magnificent dogs – their glossy black and white coats shining majestically on the canvas.

Five-year-old Bear, as his name suggests, was an enormous cuddly dog. I always called him the Cary Grant of Newfoundlands because he was so calm and polite; the perfect gentleman. He was specially trained to visit our local children's hospice, where his huggable nature made him a magnet for the love that whirls around these wonderful places.

Although Bear was a year younger than Izzie and just as placid, he was still the top dog in our house because he was…well... how would you describe him? I suppose just a massive hunk of adorable fur, in which any child would probably get lost if they cuddled too deeply.

Six-year-old Izzie was a fantastic swimmer, true to his breed. Cross-eyed as a puppy, he grew up into a confident young man. Maybe it was his Italian blood, but he was quite the Casanova and had a habit of embarrassing me big time with his amorous advances towards passing dogs, not to mention their owners and even the occasional soap star; that hilarious incident we will visit in more detail later in the book! Izzie could be a little sod, but we loved him all the same.

You're probably wondering why a hot-blooded male dog was given a girl's name. That is a question people briefly asked until it was blatantly obvious that he was not female. If you recall my infamous trip over the Clifton suspension bridge on the night of my testicle demise, Izzie's true name was Isambard, after the illustrious engineer Isambard Kingdom Brunel, who designed this glorious feat of engineering, putting Bristol well and truly on the map.

Izzie and Bear might not have achieved Brunel's level of superstardom, but they were certainly minor celebrities by 2003. Jean and I had been running our charity Newfound Friends, for fourteen years, training Newfies as water rescue dogs and then showing off their skills at festivals and sponsored events to raise money for various healthcare charities.

Our dogs, along with those of fellow Newfie owners from the region, had helped us raise £1.5 million over the years, supporting fifty-five charities, and barely a month went by when they did not appear at a fundraising event, in a newspaper, or on the TV.

Really, the last thing we needed was yet another Newfoundland dog. Then again, if Lucy was going to acquire Cracker anyway, maybe it was better the youngster came to us rather than try to stand his ground in a forty-strong pack.

"So, this go-between...?" I queried hesitantly.

"She's a respected breeder," Lucy butted in. "It's already sorted. She'll take Cracker from Monique at seven weeks, and then, if you pay the £1,500, you can have him, and I'll stay out of it until he's ready to breed. By then, Monique will just be glad he's gone to a good home."

Her tone turned silky and persuasive, if not a little false. "And you'll provide a good home, Dave; you know you will. With your training expertise and all the wonderful things you do with your charity, he'll have a fantastic life!"

I knew this was flattery, but fighting off an inner glow of self-satisfaction was difficult. "Well...I am tempted," I admitted eventually. "I am very tempted."

I glanced at Jean, who rolled her eyes but grinned in approval. She had obviously heard enough and was as cautiously thrilled about the idea as was I. Izzie and Bear looked up but kept their bellies and chins stuck to the floor, oblivious of the invasion infringing on their comfortable lives.

"Go on then," I said. "Yes. We'll do it."

That night we sat together, relaxed in front of a roaring fire, watching the flames flicker shadows across the darkened room. Raising a glass of Christmas cheer, we looked at each other, and simultaneous thoughts erupted. "Oh, God, what have we done?"

That might have been that. The decision was made, and as the days went on, enthusiasm was building for our new arrival; but it was not to be. Our exuberance was about to be shattered by an event that flew at me like a bolt of lightning, shooting me down suddenly on an otherwise clear day.

Not long after Christmas, just a few weeks after I got that phone call from Lucy, my life was flipped upside down and dragged in a dangerous new direction. Like a Lilo swept away on a rip tide – at the age of forty-seven, I almost sunk.

I had gone to see my GP for a health MOT. Although it would not be standard practice to examine my private parts, the doctor had good reason to do so because of my entanglement with Jake, the German Shepherd, a year earlier. As it turned out, had it not been for Jake's intervention in my marital apparatus, I may not be here today.

So, I was at my local surgery, trying to focus on an NHS poster on the wall and blot out the loss of dignity while he examined me below. I thought, at least it was a male doctor, and I was not having to suffer the giggles of two young nurses mocking my misfortune. Having the desired effect, a brief smile flicked across my face until it was swiftly wiped away as the doctor paused and said, "Hmm."

Yes, we've all seen it on the TV when a doctor says, 'Hmm...' he either hasn't a clue what he's doing, or you are in trouble.

"Everything okay?" I chuckled nervously. He did not reply immediately but said something diplomatic about a 'possible growth' down there and suggested I made an appointment with the oncology department at the hospital.

"It may well be nothing, but it's best to get these things checked out." I could just tell by the look on his face that all was not good.

'Right," I garbled, the blood draining from my face. "Yes, fair enough."

I didn't tell my wife and daughter about the visit to the GP. Neither did I tell them about the blood tests and biopsy

I underwent in the following days. I did not even mention my hospital appointment a few weeks later when the oncology consultant confirmed I had testicular cancer. How could I tell them something I was hardly accepting myself?

What? My first reaction was disbelief. I was in good health, or at least I'd always thought so – maybe there was some mistake. He ran me through the possible outcomes, including death, and I sat there nodding and listening with a sort of professional detachment as if he were giving me a joinery order for a staircase balustrade.

I think he said something about the 'next steps' and gave me a leaflet. By then, I had a dull ache at the back of my throat, and as I stood up, the realisation suddenly dropped through me into the pit of my stomach like hot metal. In a heartbeat, I mourned my life.

Looking back, I realize I was in shock. I drove home like a zombie, fed the dogs, and took them out for a walk. Then I cobbled together a tea for Jean and me, made some chitchat about nothing much, and went to bed.

Over the coming days and weeks, I thought of a hundred ways I could tell Jean. I practiced it over and over again, each enactment varying phrases to use; it was on the tip of my tongue every day. In the end, I gave up and hoped it might just spill out of my mouth while I was stopping Izzie from licking the walls or grabbing the drool-covered TV remote off Bear before he could chew it to bits. How could I do this? "Drop it, Bear...oh, by the way, Jean, I've got testicular cancer." How do you break it to someone you love who already has endured so much pain and discomfort?

Therefore, I never did. I do not know if that was the right decision, but it was my choice. My wife was disabled from her rheumatoid arthritis and had been in and out of hospital her whole life. There was already enough pain and anguish in our house. Anyway, I'm a joiner; I like putting stuff together. I don't like breaking stuff down and looking at it too deeply. That is why I like dogs. They get on with life, don't they until they can't go on anymore?

At home, Jean and I discussed our daughter, our dogs, and our charity – that was about it. All my hospital appointments over the following weeks took place during work when Jean thought I was at the joinery business. I drew a line in the sawdust and kept cancer out of my house.

I don't think the dogs picked up on anything before my operation, but you can never tell with Newfoundlands. After the German Shepherd attack, Izzie and Bear had certainly sniffed that something was up, probably by the whiff of local anesthetic in the air, but if they knew I had cancer, they didn't let me know.

I still took them for the same morning walks I've done for decades with all my dogs – out of the cottage, up the lane, between some houses, across a field of cows, and up to the old church of St Michael's & All Angels. With a couple of Newfoundlands on leads, it's a challenge to stay upright, never mind hold a straight line, especially when slip-sliding through muddy fields. I was always glad to let them potter on by themselves, the exuberant Izzie bounding on ahead, perhaps on the look-out for ladies, while the younger but more dignified Bear plodding along closer to me, confident that his status as a top dog was not in question.

The path follows a ridge on the southern edge of the Gordano Valley just below the lip of the M5 motorway. Above our heads, out of sight, the traffic thunders past on two concrete viaducts, the northbound some 10m higher than the southbound. Anyone who drives to and from Devon or Cornwall on their holidays will be familiar with these split sections. Next time you're passing through, look down on the valley below, and you may just spot a man out walking with his Newfoundland dogs.

Despite the roar, I still find it a peaceful place and always stop to drink in the sweeping view. There's no River Gordano, only a 'Rhyne', the old word for the drainage ditches that cross wetlands like this and the nearby Somerset

Levels. Still, it's a fine view towards the distant Welsh hills on the other side of the Bristol Channel, though the sea itself is masked from view by the side of the shallow valley.

Like always, Izzie and Bear would wait for me by the gates of the old red stone church, where I paused every morning to say my prayers and still do. The church was decommissioned in the 1990s and is now managed by a conservation trust, so the door is often locked, but the porch does me fine for the reflections I need to make. Do I believe? I think so. My family was Methodist, so, as a young boy, I had no choice but to attend church and Sunday school, and I guess my formative years left a lasting impression.

I have never asked God for things for myself, and I never will. But I suppose the routine of these morning walks was a sort of answered prayer in itself. I couldn't think of the future or plan too far ahead. I could only put one foot in front of the other, and my dogs literally dragged me through it.

When an appointment was made to remove the tumour, hoping that cancer could be caught before it spread, I told Jean I had to work away for a week, which was not unusual. It's not true, actually, that I didn't tell anyone the truth. Debbie and Sarah, fellow members of the charity Newfound Friends, came to stay for a week to help care for Jean and the dogs while I was away. Reluctantly, I decided to fill them in just in case things turned for the worst.

One thing is certain; as I turned up at the hospital for my surgery, the thought of taking on a Newfoundland puppy could not have been further from my mind. I was 100% focused on my family, dogs, carpentry business, and survival.

In fact, I'd forgotten about Cracker and my conversation with Lucy altogether – all of which had profound consequences for the dog that would one day become my beloved Whizz.

Jean, on a visit to the Oncology ward with Harry

Chapter Three: The Prince and the Pauper

I was born during a thunderstorm in September 1956, and my canine companion, Whizz, was born to the sound of fireworks on Guy Fawkes Night in 2003. You could say we both entered the world with a bang.

In order to 'Remember, remember' that very special 5th of November, his breeder Monique called him 'Fire Cracker' and his two sisters, 'Fire Blaze' and 'Fireworks'. At least she didn't call them Gunpowder, Treason, and Plot. Can you just imagine charging around a field and yelling out that lot? "Gunpowder! Treason! Plot," and to be fair, if you think about it, "Fire! Fire!" is not really much of an improvement.

Thankfully, these were only their official kennel names. Behind closed doors, Monique affectionately addressed them as Cracker, Diesel, and Daisy Moo! If you could have seen these adoring bunch of cuddly Landseer puppies, you would have known exactly why.

'Cracker', whose name would eventually be changed to Whizz, exploded into a 'cracking' start, with no effort made by himself whatsoever. He and his sisters were Newfoundland nobility and offspring of champions. Their mother was the beautiful Russian showgirl 'Humming

Chorus'; their father a handsome French stud called Gorgeous Graham, who had been paraded around the kennels of Europe like a prize bull. However, the glory of all glories were the inherited qualities of the legendary Madam Butterfly, their supreme grandmother.

Thus, Prince Whizz was treated like a royal from the moment he popped into the world at Monique's kennels in Dorset. A bundle of black and white fur with eyes tightly shut as he snuggled contently close to his mum, Whizz was totally oblivious to all the fuss surrounding his arrival. He weighed no more than a bag of sugar; yet, he was big news, and who would realize at that point in time that Whizz would turn out to be a dog in a million?

My beginnings were less auspicious. Like Whizz, I was the youngest of three, but the entry to this wonderful world was far different from that of my canine friend. No soft cushions, comfy bedding, or furry cuddles for me. I was literally born in the gutter.

I say I was the youngest of three, Marion and Richard being my older siblings, but sadly, my mother lost another baby in childbirth; who, had it survived, would have attained that title, and I would been the youngest of four. Maybe that is why she decided to choose a hospital birth for myself rather than a home delivery – which was the norm in those days.

Therefore, it was one cold, extremely wet September evening in 1956 when I chose to make my appearance, rather rapidly from all accounts, forcing the ambulance to pull over on the side of the road in Southmead, a few streets away from the hospital. I must have shot out faster than a clown desperate for a tea break catapulted at record speed from a loaded cannon.

Of course, it could have been the thunder, lightning, and torrential rain that forced the driver to stop. Either way, that's where I was delivered, in the back of an ambulance parked in the gutter of a street in north Bristol on a wild and stormy evening. I must have moved pretty quickly that night; how I wish I had that amount of energy today!

Whizz's pedigree far outshone my own. Although my paternal grandfather Christopher came from a well-to-do Bristol family, he dared to marry a miner's daughter, a girl from the Welsh valleys called Annie. His kindred thought he could do better, and after he died from inhaling gas at the Battle of Ypres in 1917, his family disowned Annie. My grandmother took on the unenviable task of bringing up one girl and seven boys alone. The eldest of these boys was my father, William (Jack).

The fate of many a family must have flipped during the world wars. Had my grandfather lived, my dad would surely have taken on his business and grown up to be a man with conservative values. Instead, he ended up taking on the responsibilities of a family at the tender age of thirteen in an era before the NHS and social security hand-outs. Scorched by injustice, he turned to the Socialist party and became a prominent trade union leader. As for my grandmother, it must have been a tremendous struggle for her, and it's to her eternal credit that all her children grew up to be good citizens.

During the Second World War, my dad was stationed at RAF Leuchars in Fife, and it was there he met my mother, Edith. She was an RAF nurse from Swansea, so I have a connection to South Wales from both parents.

Despite a bumpy birth, I had a pretty good childhood, growing up in a nice Victorian terraced house in east Bristol, close to two big parks. Dad was strict, but his trade union commitments took him away from home a lot, and my mother let me get away with blue murder. Whether it was because she'd lost a baby and almost lost me or whether it was just because I was the youngest, she made no secret of the fact that I was her favorite and pampered me rotten.

Things did not go so smoothly for Whizz. At the age of eight weeks, he was supposed to come to Jean and me via the go-between breeder that Lucy Stevenson had procured. My cancer put paid to that. I wanted to keep my privates private, so when Lucy rang me to check final arrangements, I fobbed her off with some excuse about us being too busy to take on a third dog. It was true in a way – Jean and I really did have our hands full with Izzie and Bear; besides which, they were fantastic dogs, and a third dog could have upset the dynamic. Three's a crowd and all that.

What happened next, I have pieced together from my existing knowledge of Lucy's breeding kennels and from the information she later openly admitted. How Lucy managed to acquire Whizz, I still do not fully understand, but against all odds, that is where he ended up; at her crowded home in north Devon. This was certainly against the express wishes of his owner Monique, as the two breeders were not on good terms.

Finding a loving family home for a puppy is always a difficult job, and Monique had checked and double-checked the background and credentials of the original family who were due to take on her prized puppy. When the day came to say goodbye, she was sorry to see Whizz go but confident that he was going to a calm household where he would get all the love and attention he needed.

Money and paperwork changed hands, and Whizz was driven away from his mother, his sisters, and everything he was familiar with and comfortable with. Eight weeks old, already heavier than an adult pug, he may have looked ready to take on the world, but it can take four years for a Newfie to fully mature (three years longer than a pug). He was just a baby, scared, jumpy, and vulnerable.

Instead of taking him to the owners that Monique had assiduously chosen, for some reason, it seems the go-between brought him straight to Lucy's farmhouse near Barnstaple. For Whizz, it must have been a total shock to the senses as he was led out of the van and through the yard. Metal gates scraped open and clanked shut. Blue tarpaulin sheets covering the outdoor kennels flapped and buzzed in the wind. Cages rattled as huge black, brown, and Landseer dogs pressed up against the bars, barking, growling, and sniffing at the young stranger.

Inside the farmhouse, there were dozens more dogs. The sparsely furnished dining room was full to bursting with them. In the kitchen, Whizz was greeted with a sea of furry faces as a gang of hulking Newfies hooked their enormous paws over the makeshift barrier and jostled each other for a view. Goodness knows what they smelt like to the puppy. He would have been assaulted with information about them purely from their scent – whether they were male, female, dominant, submissive, healthy, or sick. No doubt it was a sensory explosion.

Lucy, I'm sure, made Whizz feel welcome. She genuinely loved Newfoundlands, and no doubt she made a big fuss over the princely puppy she had coveted for so long. It was her passion for the breed that had led her to fill her home with the animals, after all, but the dogs would have been more suspicious. As Lucy was first and foremost a breeder, her male dogs were intact, and the females were unspayed, some carrying or nursing puppies. Despite the breed's famously friendly temperament, an outsider is an outsider, and the pack is the pack.

What those early days and nights were like for Whizz, I can only imagine. Ideally, puppies are introduced to new smells, sights, sounds, and tastes gradually in the order they have time to mentally process them and are not over-stimulated, but that was a luxury Lucy could not afford Whizz.

Usually, when a new dog arrives at our house, the first few nights are tough. The puppy cries for its mum, and I am up throughout the night trying to settle it down. Walking zombie does not even come close. Whether Lucy had the time and space to do this for Whizz, I do not know.

The kennels were well organized and clean, which is why Lucy was a successful breeder who found many happy and reputable owners over the years, including me. On the other hand, I do not see how she and her husband could possibly attend to the individual needs of thirty-five to forty dogs, particularly the young ones. The maths does not add up; even if she had limited their walks to one half-hour outing a day and taken five at a time (a feat in itself that was well within Lucy's capabilities), that was still four hours of work!

Adding to this arduous task, the daily routine of feeding, cleaning up, and grooming three dozen enormous animals takes forever. On top of this, there would be essential care required for the pregnant bitches and their litters, regular trips to the vets, and organising the stud services of her males. Lucy also had to find the time to attend dog shows with her favorites. How would there be time to even eat or go to the toilet? I do not know.

Pack dynamics were another challenge. With so many females coming in and out of season and so many males vying for their attention, Lucy's home must have constantly felt like kicking out time at a nightclub, with all the drama that brings. After a night out on the tiles, feisty humans strutting their 'stuff' (or more likely stumbling off the kerb in a drunken stupor) would be on the hunt for amorous conquest.

If you were a dog, you would be parading dominantly round the yard, holding your head high, shaking your long shaggy locks, and drooling your slobbery chops. 'Look at me, aren't I just so... irresistible?' Punch-ups between both sets of Casanovas were almost unavoidable.

There is no way she and her husband could have broken up a fight between two thirteen-stone hairy love rivals; it was crucial to anticipate flash points and separate dogs that did not get along. Eventually, the rebellious canines will establish their place in the social hierarchy and organize themselves into a peaceful pack. Newfoundlands, who are generally a laid-back bunch and particularly adept at this within their family groups, but unlike the others, young Whizz had no blood relations in the pack. With neither his mum nor his dad to vouch for him, he did not belong, and increasingly, he was separated from the others in order to keep the peace.

It is heart-breaking to think of Whizz being left on his own. Just as with humans, the first two years of a puppy's life are a critical period that hugely influences the way they cope with the world in the future. And like our children, they thrive on play and social interaction and respond positively to boundaries, encouragement, and love.

Isolated from the close-knit pack, Whizz began to live up to the outcast role imposed upon him; he became disruptive and destructive. On walks, he snapped and snarled at other dogs and tried to escape at every conceivable opportunity. In his shed, he ripped toys to shreds along with anything else he could destroy with his gnashers to relieve his boredom. In short, unless he received the attention he deserved, he was well on his way to becoming a juvenile delinquent.

It must have been distressing for Lucy. A few times, she considered selling Whizz, but she had such high hopes for this pedigree puppy and badly wanted to mate him with the right female. Her kennels could then play a part in his prestigious dynasty. Under Kennel Club rules, however, Whizz could not be mated until he was aged at least two, and by this stage, he was only a few months old.

Pedigree dogs are particularly vulnerable to hereditary health conditions such as hip and elbow dysplasia and heart and eye problems; Newfoundlands are no different. These conditions can only be tested properly in a mature dog, so it's very important to abide by the two-year rule, though some breeders get around it with convenient 'accidental' litters.

As time went on, Whizz was growing fast but confined more and more to the loneliness of the shed at the back of the yard. Lucy's grandchildren would sometimes visit him, eager to play with the puppy. However, each time he was brought out of solitary confinement, there was always drama whenever he mixed with the other dogs. Thus, the opportunities became few and far between – Whizz was in limbo – it was a very sad state of affairs.

My own life was on hold too, but just as things were starting to look really bleak for Whizz, I was thrown a lifeline. My testicular cancer was caught early, and the surgery was a success. After a course of pioneering drugs from the States, the doctors thankfully told me that I was going to make it.

The relief was immense. To be honest, I was only just holding it together. Jean was not well, and I was struggling to keep on top of the joinery business, honoring the many contracts with looming penalty clauses whilst also trying to run the Newfound Friends charity with my wife.

Although I was still aiming to keep cancer a secret, Newfoundlands are a presumptive breed, and I am sure Izzie and Bear were unsettled, intuitively suspecting something was amiss. Swimming was out of bounds, and our dog walks were slower and shorter than before, both things the boys would have picked up on.

By this time, I had forgotten all about the Landseer puppy I'd been offered a year earlier. I had no idea that Cracker had ended up at Lucy's kennels and been renamed Whizz or what his unfortunate situation was – that is, until one morning in December 2004, a couple of months after doctors had given me the all-clear. Completely out of the blue, I received a phone call from Lucy.

"He's a nightmare, Dave," she admitted. "A really difficult dog."

I couldn't answer at first. My mind was galloping at nineteen to the dozen, mentally processing the fact that she owned Whizz in the first place. How on earth had she got hold of him? Monique had been so vehemently against the idea.

"Oh?" I said finally.

Lucy told me everything; her high hopes for his arrival, her dismay at his failure to mix with the rest of the pack, and her gradual realisation that he would have to go.

"Where do you keep him then?" I queried.

"In a shed in the yard mostly."

"On his own?" I tried not to sound dismayed.

"He upsets the other dogs and bares his teeth at them," she babbled defensively. "There's no way I can let him mix with the others – no way; it would be a bloodbath." She sounded genuinely despaired. "I've tried. But he's really, really, difficult."

I cast my mind back to when my own Newfoundlands were puppies and tried to imagine them languishing alone in a shed for long periods of time. It would have been intolerable to be separated from other dogs, myself and Jean, yet able to see, hear and smell us. Yep, of course, he was difficult. Anyone, human or animal, would be, stuck in a cage on their own. Lucy knew why and I also knew it was not rocket science. He was bored, under-socialised, fearful, depressed, and, yeah, difficult, just like a child isolated from mortal interaction. No wonder he was aggressive.

Truly dominant dogs rarely go on the attack. You only had to look at Bear to see that. He was the alpha canine in our house, yet soft as you like. No, an aggressive dog is, more often than not, an anxious dog, a dog that has to get the first snarl in before others notice – that it's actually lacking in confidence.

"Why don't you just sell him on?" I suggested.

There was an awkward silence on the line, and I could sense that Lucy was choosing her words carefully. "Because I wanted to... I mean, the whole point was to… I did try him out with one of my bitches in the season back in the summer."

I was dumbstruck. She'd tried to mate him back in the summer when he was only eight months old!

"And?" I resisted the urge to snarl like the animal to which she referred.

"It didn't work," replied Lucy. "He was a dead loss, really."

Blood rose to my face. A dead loss? He must have been terrified. I was trying to summon the words to give Lucy a piece of my mind when she put her cards on the table.

"Anyway," she continued with some displacency. "I've got to let him go. He was supposed to go to you in the first place, so if you want him, you can have him."

I closed my eyes. Poor dog. I wanted to help, but I was wary. A year earlier, Whizz would have been an impressionable puppy, responsive to training and able to grow up as part of our family. Now he was a 'difficult' one-year-old that clashed with other dogs. Maybe it was too late.

"I don't know, Lucy," I said hesitantly. "I need to think about Bear and Izzie. And Jean's not in the best health at the moment…"

"Or if you can think of anyone else who'd want him," Lucy butted in, with more than an edge of desperation in her voice. "It would have to be on the proviso that I can mate him in the future, mind. That would have to be written into the contract."

I flinched. If I could see her, I was sure her eyes would be lit up with pound signs and pinging up and down like the potential jackpot on a one-arm bandit.

"Oh, I don't know about that," I retorted.

"No!" My fierce reaction surprised even me. "If I took him on, that would be that. I wouldn't be happy with anyone breeding from him."

There was silence on the line for a few moments, and I sensed Lucy's mind ticking over.

Finally, she sighed in retreat. "So, you'll take him on then?"

Jean wasn't there to consult; I had to make a snap decision. "Let's meet up," I eventually said. "If you bring him to the Cotswold Lake, we'll take a look at him…"

I could sense Lucy's mood brighten instantly. "You'll love him," she gushed. "He's a stunning specimen, as handsome as your Bear. You'll be bowled over when you see him. And remember, he was meant to come to you and Jean in the first place."

That much was true, Whizz had been destined to come to us as an infant, but like pieces of wood falling off a workbench, both our lives had been splintered and thrust way off course.

My grandfather, who died in the trenches, as I said, was also a joiner. The First World War decided his destiny, and he was never able to pursue his ambitions, preventing my father from taking on his joinery business. Half a century later, I relit the fire and also became a joiner founding my own business. Like my grandfather before me, no doubt, I relished that piecing feeling when you achieve a neat fit. I thought about Whizz and his jumbled-up existence... maybe fate was sending him to us, and maybe... our lives were intended to dovetail.

"Okay," I replied. "But I'm not promising anything."

"Okay," Lucy repeated my agreement, with some relief I felt.

I had tried to sound uncommitted throughout the conversation, but deep down, I somehow knew that Whizz was meant for us.

David with Izzie and Bear at the national dog trainer of the year award. Held at the Dorchester hotel Mayfair London

Chapter Four: Omega Male

It was a mild but drizzly winter afternoon and the last training session of the year at our lake in the Cotswolds. We were all used to miserable weather, but it did not bother our brave Newfies, who were enthusiastic to leap into the water and do their job. As for us? Obviously, we would have preferred to splash around on a lovely summer's day, soaking up the warmth of the sun; and we did have our moments of fun and frolics. Horseplay with the dogs was thoroughly enjoyable; 'horseplay' was a very appropriate description bearing in mind the size of our canine friends. Ultimately, however, besides this joyful side to our group, the charity objectives were, more importantly, about support, aid, and rescue. Training was essential to ensure safety for all people and animals involved.

Unfortunately, Jean, with her painful conditions, could not cope with the damp, and on this occasion, much as she would have liked to greet our newcomer, she had reluctantly decided to stay at home. The word had spread fast of this new majestic arrival, and thus, plenty of other Newfound Friends members had turned up for the momentous occasion.

By the time Lucy's car pulled into the car park, a small throng had gathered, eager to catch a glimpse of Newfie royalty. An experienced dog handler in her sixties', Lucy strode around the car, her long white hair swept into a ponytail, swinging from side to side in the breeze. Opening the passenger door, she looked at Whizz, then at the audience. A look at the pair from the crowd was enough, everyone realized that Whizz needed some space, and sensibly all backed away.

My destiny was too scared to emerge; the black and white creature stirred and turned his doleful eyes towards me but did not budge.

I was expecting to be literally knocked over by a large, boisterous bundle of enveloping fur with heartthrob looks and a princely swagger. 'Stunning', Lucy had called him. 'As handsome as Bear', she had promised... 'My Destiny'; but here he was, a scared little church mouse, frightened to emerge from the pew.

Slotting a lead onto Whizz's collar, gently encouraging response, Lucy calmly uttered, "Come on, out you get, darling."

A delicate tug finalised the task, and the confused youngster clambered hesitantly out. His tail hung low, and his facial expression was bleak as he plumaged into the gravel. My heart sank; he was a sorry sight, scrawny and unsure of himself.

"Hello, Whizz?" I welcomed him with somewhat trepid enthusiasm. Moving my hand slowly, I smoothed his glossy black head and gave him a tickle behind the ears. It certainly did not look like I was at any risk of being licked to death, let alone knocked off my feet. 'On his level, it is then', I decided, calmly dropping onto one knee and giving his neck and shoulders a friendly rub.

Whizz fixed me with treacle eyes and gingerly sniffed my face, no doubt picking up the scent of our more confident dogs. Almost nose to nose, I felt his hot panting breath easing as I noticed the white streak that ran upwards to his forehead, crowned with a star on the top of his black head – he was indeed a king. "Alright, boy?" I murmured. "Fancy a swim?"

Having been training all morning with Izzie and Bear, who were drying off in the van, I was already kitted out in my semi-dry suit and boots – I would not have to leave Whizz and disturb this initial interaction. Thus, I decided, a tentative dip in the lake seemed a good way to put him at ease. After all, what Newfie could resist the call of liquid gold? Right...

With Lucy by my side, I led Whizz down to the lake shallows. Most Newfoundlands have an instinctive desire to swim and will go charging into the water with their ears bouncing and tails whirling. Not so Whizz –I guessed he had not even been allowed near a garden pond before (knowing his told character, carp would be on the menu); he almost certainly would never have swum in, or possibly seen, such a vast expanse of H_2O.

Pausing at the lake's edge, his nose pushed forward and gave the water a cagey sniff as if to say, "This doesn't smell like the stuff in my bowl. What the hell is it, and is it going to poison me?"

After unhooking his lead, I waded in up to my thighs, then crouched down, bore a toothy grin, and called out: "Come on, Whizz!"

He padded two massive front paws up and down with an air of anxiety, then, eventually, ventured forward, tentatively, into the drink.

"Come on, Whizz! We will fight them on the beaches!" I was sure once he was in, he would be off like a shot.

Not so Whizz – he did a half-hearted paddle in the shallows with all the enthusiasm of a grudging teenager, bribed to do something embarrassing by his dad. Within a minute or two, he was out and legging it back to safety.

Maybe swimming wasn't for him, I thought, as he shook his coat and hung his head. Maybe he wasn't cut out for the life of a Newfound Friends water rescue dog. Fair enough; animals are individuals, just like humans, and you can't force them to be something they're not.

Although it was hard to swallow my disappointment, I realized I had been daydreaming something completely different. I thought the thrill of swirling around in the water might awaken something natural in Whizz, and he would emerge from the lake bouncing and barking for joy. I saw it all, a magical, born-again Newfie on the path to becoming my best-ever water rescue dog.

'Yeah, right, mister. Like that's gonna happen', Whizz seemed to tell me as we wandered back to the car park. Wet through and bedraggled, he looked more downcast than a depressed duckling, failing its first attempt at fulfilling the expectation of life.

"So, do you want him then?" asked Lucy. Gone was the empathy for the sad-looking creature plonked beside me. she sounded desperate to get shot of him and more concerned about the five-hour round trip from north Devon to Fairford in Gloucestershire.

"Let's see what the others say," I replied, still conveying my lack of commitment.

By 'the others', I meant Bear and Izzie. As for myself? I think then; I knew deep inside that I was not going to give up on this dog. However, I am a great believer in letting dogs sort things out for themselves, and when it came to deciding whether or not to extend our family, I decided my two boys should have the casting vote. 'Two's company and three's a crowd' and all that... but when you are talking dogs... BIG dogs... the jostling for attention is likely to be worse than a fight for first place in the queue to nab the last burger on sale at Glastonbury music festival.

The meeting was approached with both hope and apprehension. The 'boys' were still happily lolling around in the van when I walked my new companion to the vehicle and slid open the door. Telling Bear and Izzie they had a visitor, I encouraged the outsider to enter, crossing more than my fingers and toes and holding my breath. After all, Whizz was apparently a 'difficult' character that clashed with other dogs, and if things were going to turn nasty, it could be sudden and brutal.

Whizz kept his tail down in supplication and allowed himself to be sniffed and evaluated. I closed the side door and watched through the open rear doors, safely screened by a strong metal grille.

To my relief, the van did not shake, rattle or roll. There were no growls or whines of alarm. While not exactly smothering him in kisses, Izzie and Bear seemed to return a favourable verdict. That is when I cemented my decision to pay Lucy the £1,600 and take the poor boy home. This may seem little to pay for a top pedigree Newfoundland, but this would be equivalent to around £5000 nowadays – a fair old price to pay!

The journey back to North Somerset was far more peaceful than I could have anticipated. I kept my ears primed for trouble in the rear of the van, but there was not a whimper. I was hoping that was a good sign and not that all three of them were pinned separately against the sides, glaring at each other, planning an assault at the right 'time and place'.

Mind you; I bet Whizz took one look at Bear and thought, "I ain't gonna take you on; you're bleedin' massive – not sure I fancy the big furry sidekick much either!"

Izzie, reliant on Bear's protection, would have hissed, "Ain't you gonna show him who's boss then?"

Bear, who was supremely confident in his pack leader status and a laid-back dog at that, probably gave Whizz a pitying look and piped up to his brother in arms: "Don't need to do I? He's no alpha male. More like an omega male!"

Although I could not deny my immediate connection with Whizz, it was hard to shake off my disappointment with Whizz's poor condition and his lacklustre dip in the lake.

How would a non-swimming Newfoundland fit into our family when so much of our lives revolved around a water rescue charity?

As I drove Whizz, Bear, and Izzie home to North Somerset that afternoon in December 2004, proud memories flooded my mind of the successes of Newfound Friends. I thought of the dogs we had trained, the rescues, the awards, and most of all, the looks of enjoyment on the faces of all the people we had helped and given an element of light relief, even if just for a day. How great it would be if we could continue the successes with Whizz... At that moment in time, my aspirations were doused.

After parking up outside our cottage and closing the gates, I opened the side door of the van and let the dogs out. Izzie and Bear knew the routine – jumping down and strolling into the house, nonchalantly cocking their legs over my prize flower-pots on the way in, as was the time-honored tradition. Of course, my blooms did not ever get a sniff of an entry to any competition. The only thing they were fit for after being continually attacked by acid rain was the compost heap at the end of the garden.

Whizz followed the confident boys at a deferential distance but hesitated as he neared the open door as if expecting to be attacked for his audacity.

"Come on in, Whizz," I gently said, stepping inside the house and giving him a reassuring rub behind the ears. He looked up at me and took a step forward but then seemed to change his mind and backed off, tail between his legs. To him, the place must have looked enormous and intimidating.

I am a great believer in leaving dogs to do things at their own pace, so I left the door open and went to sort out a meal for Bear and Izzie. After their long day at the training lake, they were ravenous and scoffed down their cooked chicken in moments.

"Did you bring him home or not?'" asked Jean, looking around for the new member of our family.

I pointed through the window to the garden where Whizz was still wandering around in circles, tentatively exploring the aroma of vegetation.

"He looks a bit skinny, poor fella," frowned Jean. "Has he had anything to eat?"

I shook my head and explained the events of the day. While she listened, Jean unwrapped some large chicken pieces from the fridge. Tiptoeing into the garden in her slippers, she dangled the tasty morsels close to Whizz's nose, uttering encouraging murmurs to calm and coax him into the house. Finally, her patience paid off, and Whizz slowly padded inside. Food works wonders, and as soon as he spied a bowl full of tempting premium dog food set out for him at head height, speed suddenly exploded, and he dived in, wolfing it down in a few seconds flat.

That night, as Bear and Izzie settled down in the kitchen, as usual, Whizz retreated into a corner under the table. It must have been the safest refuge he could find after a long day of strange goings-on. And I hoped the kitchen tiles would feel comfortable and cool under his belly.

Whizz was not the only one to feel tired. I retired to my bed with a mixture of relief and anxiousness in my mood. Thankfully, and rather surprisingly, I slept well and was undisturbed by any whimpering or argy-bargy. But could it last?

Izzie ready for his adventure in Southern Ireland

Chapter Five: Big Pawprints to Fill

Whizz spent most of his first weekend hiding under the kitchen table. He was on edge and subdued, shying away from myself, Jean, and the other dogs. Even though his previous confinement was totally miserable, I could only imagine how he was feeling to be wrenched away from all familiar.

Kind words, patience, and understanding were given in abundance, along with the temptation of the most delicious tender meats, in order to coax him from within his chosen comfort zone.

Initially, a walk was out of the question. It is certainly no picnic, slip-sliding along a muddy path with three restrained, galumphing Newfies. Many a time, I have escaped soggy demise managing the trio, let alone another jittery companion. More importantly, of course, the disruption of routine for the pack may prove too much too soon and certainly cause Whizz further distress.

Things stayed on a pretty even keel those first two days until Monday morning when I set off for work, leaving Jean in charge. I refrained from fussing Whizz, thinking it would be best to leave him to emerge when he saw fit. It turned out

I had completely underestimated his reaction to my disappearance.

I had not been at the joiner's yard long and focusing my mind on the task at hand when the call came...

"Dave, you need to come home... now!"

My heart missed a beat, "What's happened? Are you okay?"

"I'm fine," said Jean. "But it's all kicking off here."

"Where's Whizz?"

"He's... um... he's wearing the kitchen table."

If it had not been for the hint of panic in her voice, I could have sensed a slight indication of amusement.

"Eh?"

"Just come quick!"

Shoving my carpentry masterpiece aside, I rapidly vacated the premises and dashed home. It was hard to concentrate on driving, imagining what mayhem had erupted in my absence.

I arrived to find Izzie and Bear contained in the garden, the sorrowful lack of eye contact and the sheepish look on their faces told all. As I let myself in and walked through the living room toward the kitchen, I heard a thud – Whizz's head hitting the table as he made his escape. This was swiftly followed by the scuffle of flying paws as the young but huge canine scrabbled across the kitchen tiles.

I barely had time to catch my breath before the big furry bulldozer came hurtling down the hallway to greet me. Plonking his front paws firmly on my shoulders, slobbery pants huffing in my face, his tail karate chopped in triumph. How I stood my ground and avoided being flattened into a trampled cardboard box, I will never know.

"Alright, Whizz," I soothed. "Alright, down, boy – down."

Eventually, my new friend condescended to release his grip and remove his torso from my body. I do not think he had any idea of the chaos that surrounded his actions. Whizz just looked up with big soppy eyes, cocked his head as if to say, 'What's the problem? I just need a bit of a cuddle!'

In the kitchen, Jean was clearing up a scene of mild destruction; a couple of broken mugs, a chair knocked to the floor; papers were strewn across the floor; the place looked like the aftermath of a pooch party rave.

Jean told me Whizz had seemed jumpy after my departure and backed himself into a corner under the kitchen table. Bear and Izzie, wondering what was up with their new housemate, had decided to investigate, following him into his hiding place. I guess they only wanted to have some fun with their new acquaintance, but Whizz saw them as a threat, spooked, and growled in defence.

"The other two didn't get it," explained Jean. "They thought it was all a game."

I surveyed the scene; it resembled the aftermath of a cafe brawl, and I wondered, 'who won?'

It took several weeks to convince Whizz that he was part of the family, that if I went out to work, I would come home again, that if I went out into the garden, I would come in again, that if I went to the toilet – well, you get the picture. I was careful not to fuss over him too much in front of Bear and Izzie, as I did not want to stoke any jealousy. However, whenever their backs were turned, I would ruffle the fur on my companion's neck, smoothing his cheeks to gently alleviate the anxiety, trying to convince him he was alright and that he was 'my Whizz'.

"You're alright, boy," I'd soothe, over and over. "You're home now – you're home."

I guess Whizz was used to being pushed from pillar to post. Being previously rejected by a forty-strong pack, why would Bear and Izzie be any different? How could he possibly have known that he would not be alienated and moved on yet again?

Bear and Izzie were different, though. For starters, Bear was too massive to invade Whizz's safe space. He had already learned from bitter experience that if he fancied a trip under the kitchen table, he would end up taking it for an outing around the room, sending knives, forks, mugs, and the teapot flying in all directions. Besides, Bear was pretty much a great big softie who had nothing to prove; therefore, he quickly bonded with the Newfie newcomer.

Had the more gregarious Izzie still been in his prime, the feisty animal may have picked a fight or two with the young upstart, but then, our Italian stallion was advancing towards the end of his life, unfortunately suffering from a condition called laryngeal paralysis, which prevented his vocal cords functioning properly and gave him breathing problems. Thus, he looked upon Whizz without intolerance.

I often noticed Whizz watching our two boys as they ambled around the garden together or crept into Jean's ensuite bathroom to get a swig of water from the loo. I never really understood why they would choose to sink their faces into such an unsavoury place when there were tempting bowls of fresh cool water luxuriously placed on head-height drinking stands. It was all set out as a posh hotel bar, yet they would happily walk straight past, with snobby noses in the air, and make a beeline for the toilet.

Dogs are pack animals, and there is little you can teach them that they cannot learn from each other. To understand what made Whizz the amazing dog he turned out to be, you really need to know the stories of his adopted brothers...

Izzie's Tale

Izzie cost me a staircase and two window frames. Most people in Newfie circles know of my joinery business, so when a breeder contacted me in 1997 to place an order, we came to an arrangement. No money changed hands, but the old bartering system flew into action, and when his next bundle of Landseer puppies arrived, I was promised one from the litter.

The son of an Italian stud, Izzie was a cross-eyed black and white puppy and not the most handsome or biggest Newfoundland, but by gosh, he could swim to perfection. When Bear came along a year later, he, too, became a proficient water rescue dog, but Izzie always had that edge. He was a flamboyant adrenaline junkie, and if he had been human, he would certainly have hosted an extreme sports TV show or something equally as exciting.

Throughout his ten-year life, Izzie certainly enjoyed more than your average fifteen minutes of fame. His time in the limelight really took off after the Animal Health Trust

Awards for talented dogs in 1990. We both received awards that day; Izzie for his achievements and myself for 'Dog Trainer of The Year'; It was one of the greatest moments of my life. I remember that ceremony, particularly because, strangely, even though the actual event was geared up for the dogs, they weren't actually allowed into the venue.

Therefore, Izzie and Bear were looked after by veterinary nurses while I went into the Hilton Mayfair hotel and mingled with an eye-popping A-list of the glitterati. Included in this group of celebrities were Sean Connery and Michael Caine, not that I spoke to them; I was too busy fretting over how the veterinary nurses would be coping with Izzie. He could be a real handful at the best of times, and if he even whiffed a sniff of a vet, there was trouble!

The talent award was a fantastic honor and opened the door to a wealth of opportunities for our charity, Newfound Friends. One TV production company came all the way from Canada to film Izzie in action for a documentary (or should I say, 'dogumentary'?) about working dogs called K9 to Five.

The filming went well until the crew realized that they had forgotten to bring an underwater camera to capture Izzie's powerful swimming stroke. They were all stood there umming and ahhing – striding aimlessly around, staring into outer-space like lost sheep wondering why the shepherd had disappeared, when the cameraman broke the silence and came up with an ingenious idea.

What the local pet shop owner thought when he strode into the store and asked for a fish tank to use for a swimming dog, I dread to think; one could only imagine his garbled response of "What size did you have in mind?"

It did, however, turn out to be a brilliant plan. Partially submerging it in the water, keeping the camera beneath the surface but dry, worked a treat. The submarine shots of Izzie swimming were a highlight of the program!

Izzie's next big break was in promotion. We were approached by one of the very top advertising companies, asking if they could use him to promote a new brand of dog food that apparently reduced tartar on dogs' teeth.

Jean was horrified when I told her what they were planning. "You what?" she cried. "They want him to jump out of a helicopter? Are you having me on?"

Nope, they were serious! The agency wanted a high-octane sequence to grab the viewers' attention. My first thought was 'not bloody likely'. What if it was too far for Izzie to jump? What if he caught his leg on the helicopter's landing skids on the way down? What if the down-draught from the helicopter blades made the sea too choppy? What if the noise from the engines caused him distress? A million reasons to refuse were swarming my brain.

Then, I found Mike Thompson, a pilot in Cornwall who was well respected in the film industry. He owned a Dolphin helicopter with a retractable undercarriage, meaning no metal for Izzie to catch himself on. Mike had bags of experience, and thankfully, one by one, he addressed all my anxieties until there was just one hurdle: the UK Aviation Authority would not sanction a loose animal in an aircraft of any kind.

The only way around the problem was to shoot the scene in Ireland. The producers chose the aptly named location Dog's Bay, a spectacular sheltered cove in County Galway with white sands, turquoise waters, and not a rock in sight.

Izzie and I arrived the evening before filming and slept in the van on the beach. I say, 'slept, with gritted teeth'. With Izzie snoring away and pawing me frequently in the face, shuteye evaded my weary body. The next morning, I emerged bleary-eyed into the sunshine while he was typically all bright and breezy.

We filmed some easier sequences first; then, in the afternoon, it was time for our leap of faith. Izzie and I were strapped into the chopper, Mike lifted off, and before we knew it, we were looking down on the clear waters of Dog's Bay.

Mike had an aircraft technician with him to calculate the distance he could safely fly over the sea and to hold onto Izzie while I jumped. I have to say, looking down onto the ocean being churned up by the downdraft of the chopper blades, my heart was thudding like a clapped-out lawnmower. As much as the negative thought 'I wish I had never agreed to this bloody thing' was flooding through my head, with the advertising agency's nineteen-strong entourage watching my every move, there was no turning back.

Straight legs together, arms rigidly at my sides, I dropped into the sea like a lead shot and bobbed back up a few moments later. There was no time to feel relieved; Izzie would only be allowed to jump if I was totally confident it was safe. I looked up to the helicopter – the distance was no more than two point five meters. Izzie had jumped greater distances from quaysides. I was confident he could do it and gave the thumbs up.

Mike took the aircraft round the bay and carefully manoeuvred the helicopter back into position while I began splashing and flailing like a drowning man. On a discreet signal, Izzie was set free. My daredevil dog didn't hesitate for a second; I will never forget that silhouette as he soared through the air like a shaggy Superman, landing by my side with a great splash. "That's my boy!" I breathed.

I could not help but feel a bit emotional as he towed me nonchalantly back to the beach, where I staggered onto the sand, feeling exhausted but utterly triumphant. That feeling fizzled fast when the producer asked us to do another take.

Fortunately, Izzie did me proud the second time, and thank goodness, Mike saved us from the threat of a third take by reminding the finance director how much his helicopter expenses would be!

I was told the commercial aired on American television, and the manufacturers were thrilled with the results. To ensure the advertisement was genuine, and as a thank you, they shipped a container of dog food for Izzie to devour. Unfortunately, it was ceased by customs as it was unlicensed in the UK; thus, he never got to taste the meaty feast. Maybe that was just as well, as I am not sure where we would store a container full of dog food... they must have thought we lived on a massive farm with loads of outbuildings. I had intended to donate a few tins to the local dog sanctuary; what a waste of food. I always wondered where it all ended up, certainly legally disposed of, but, just in case, I wouldn't have bought any takeaways for a few weeks if I lived near the port!

Every celebrity has a cringe moment that is splashed across the tabloids, and it was only a matter of time for a hairy extrovert like Izzie to claim his moment of fame.

In the year 2000, he was awarded his first (and only) solo trophy at the Golden Bone Awards for his services in enhancing the lives of mankind. It was a star-studded ceremony held at the fancy Kensington Roof Gardens and hosted by the TV sports presenter Sue Barker.

The grandeur of the occasion was completely lost on Izzie, who was bored with all the razzmatazz and was itching to go home. There was just the final, obligatory, photographic session with the press, who were lined up ready to unleash (if you pardon the pun) their artistic talents.

Eventually, our turn arrived, and we were paired with soap star Wendy Richards. Ms Richards was famous for her role as Pauline Fowler in Eastenders, but her career was long and varied. She starred in many comic movies, including, in her younger days, roles in the 'Carry on' films. Her TV debut really kicked off when she landed a part as Miss Brahms in the 1970's sitcom 'Are you being Served'. Sadly, she is no longer with us.

I had noticed Wendy had been smoking through a cigarette holder throughout the evening. I did wonder if that was a sign that the lady was, to coin a phrase, 'a bit of a diva'. However, as it turned out, she had had a tooth extracted earlier that day, and I could not have been more wrong in my perceptions.

The dozen or so assembled snappers were anxious to obtain photographs of Wendy, cuddling up to 'loveable' Izzie. Unfortunately, my faithful companion was bored out of his big socks and refused to look at the camera. This resorted in me jumping up and down like a demented medicine man, trying to gain his attention – without success.

Izzie, 'loveable' in more ways than one, decided that Wendy was the dish of the day and not a bunch of wild horses was going to stop his amorous intentions. Before anyone could intervene, my naughty dog had pushed the unsuspecting conquest to the floor and proceeded to mount the poor fifty-seven-year-old woman.

Wendy was trying, and miserably failing, to fend off Casanova, whilst I fought desperately to push through the wall of photographers – not a dog in hell's chance – they were ecstatic to obtain such a scoop!

The embarrassment on my face was evident; the whole incident could not have been worse. As for Wendy? Whether it was her history with filming the mildly raunch Carry-on scenes or the innuendos constantly aired in the series 'Are You Being Served', I do not know, but she thought it all absolutely hilarious and laughed it all off.

The headlines splashed across the front page of the red-tops the following day were classic. 'Beast-Ender' from the Mirror and 'Oops! Pauline on her bark-side' from the Daily Star. Of course, the organizers were thrilled with the coverage; not sure about Wendy; then again, no publicity is bad publicity and all that.

So, that was our Izzie; a real handful at times, but also a strong, brave, fantastic swimmer who was up for it at any time... in more ways than one!

Bear's story

Hefty but humble, that was Bear. While Izzie was out there wowing the crowds and wooing soap stars, Bear was plodding along in the background, quietly winning hearts. He was the epitome of the gentle giant, a fourteen-stone softie with large, soulful big eyes oozing pools of shimmering oil. Wispy tufts of dark fluff protruded waywardly upward from his majestic black head. Even positioned securely on all four legs, he stood shoulder to shoulder with most of the kids he met. They were rarely intimidated, and such was Bear's gentle demeanour. If any of the children asked nicely, he would lift a mighty white paw to shake their hand, like the perfect gentleman he was.

Our greatest water rescue dogs have always had a slight edge to them, but there were no such traits with Bear, and I am proud to say he was the first dog in the UK to be accredited by a national body as a companion for terminally ill children.

I didn't actually pay for Bear, either. He was bought for Newfound Friends by a wonderful, kind-hearted couple from Oxfordshire; Christine and Richard Newett. To be honest, I was wary when they got in touch one day in 1998 and asked if they could buy our charity a dog. It was only when Jean and I met them that we understood.

Each year, the Newetts would forgo Christmas, birthday, and anniversary presents, asking friends and family to donate money instead to fund a specialist service dog. Over the years, they had provided guide dogs, hearing dogs for the deaf, and other therapy support canines. This year they chose, wonderfully, to approach us.

At the time, Newfound Friends was regularly raising money for Little Bridge House, the first ever children's hospice in the Southwest of England. Jean and I often visited with our other Newfoundland Harry, who we were blessed with at the time. However, he was 'getting on a bit', to say the least, and deserved a well-earned retirement. It occurred to us that maybe we could train a puppy as a companion dog for terminally ill children.

With a blank cheque, we took our time to find the perfect puppy, and I knew as soon as I clapped eyes on Bear, curled up on the sofa with the owner's granddaughter, that he was the one.

Before we could take Bear into a hospice setting, his temperament had to be assessed. This was carried out by the experts at 'Pets as Therapy', a wonderful national charity whose accredited animals go into hospitals, care homes, prisons, and schools. Bear was methodically put through his paces to check he could walk on a relaxed lead, accept being prodded and patted, and cope with sudden noises and disturbances. Jumping up was not allowed, and we were told Bear would fail the test if he pawed, barked, growled, licked, snatched, or backed away when petted.

We were proud to see he passed with flying colours, and it was only a matter of weeks before he made his debut at Little Bridge House. The hospice in North Devon is an amazing place; far more than an establishment to administer care and support for terminally ill youngsters in their final moments. It is also a loving home-from-home for whole families, where everyone can relax and enjoy some respite.

Nurses and carers are in attendance twenty-four hours a day and attentive to every need. Everyone goes out of their way to ensure an abundance of fun activities are fully accessible. Families get to spend more quality time, not only with sick children but also with healthy siblings who may have missed out on attention.

As a puppy, Bear was as big as a sheep; we were mindful not to go barging into the hospice like a... well... like a bear. We stayed mainly around the gardens or in the conservatory for our visits. Most people, though – kids, parents, and staff alike – just wanted to throw their arms around Bear and sink their cheeks into his fur; he was basically a walking pillow.

You would be forgiven for thinking the sight of an enormous Bear plodding across the lawn would be intimidating; after all, Newfoundlands are strong enough to break through ice in Arctic seas, but this amazing creature had an immense, calming aura about him. His presence lifted dark spirits and sparked curious and excited babble. No introductions or encouragement were ever necessary.

Jean often came on trips to Little Bridge House. She knew what it was like to have the rug pulled from under your feet and to live with pain. It was not our place to intrude or comment on the children or parents concerning the personal circumstances that had brought them to the hospice. Our job was to guide families away from all that, even if for a little while, and let the dogs do the talking. Occasionally we saw tears, but mostly it was huge amounts of fun and lots of laughter.

Particularly with assistance dogs, I have always thought it's the dog itself that changes a person's life, not the job it is trained to do. A dog can be taught to guide a blind person across a road or place the clothes belonging to a disabled person in the washing machine. These are incredible skills, but the critical thing is the dog's need for love and exercise.

That inescapable fact means owners are blessed with a faithful companion, hopefully for life, providing motivation to venture outside, to feel sun and rain on their faces, and enjoy the fresh air. The benefits to the human mind and health are immense, not forgetting the highlight of the day for our furry friends, who thrive on the exercise and thrill of the environment. How can they resist the pet of a compassionate hand or the attention of a playful acquaintance... and, of course, those scrummy treats hidden unsuccessfully in deep pockets?

The social aspect is of equal importance – a dog is a great instigator of conversation. People will stop to admire and fuss over a friendly animal, facilitating light-hearted banter and chit-chat of the day. Loneliness can be relieved and low moods eradicated; friendships may blossom, bonds cemented. In fact, to put it into a few words – the greatest thing a dog can do is just be a dog!

It was a privilege to be invited into the lives of the families and staff at the hospice. A couple, whom we will never forget, struck up a long-lasting friendship with us; their names were Marie and Peter Budd. They had two terminally ill sons, Daniel and Adam, together with a healthy daughter called Natalia. The whole family just clicked with Bear, particularly Natalia, who was so taken with him and went on to train with the dogs and raise thousands of pounds for the charity.

As with Izzie in his role for services to people, Bear was so successful in his work with terminally ill children that he was awarded a gold medal in 2002 for 'Pets Therapy Dog of the Year', and another in 2004, being 'The Daily Mail Dog of the Year'. He was also nominated for another prestigious decoration and was to be presented at the Golden Bone Awards. I invited the Budds to accompany me to the ceremony.

The awards evening itself was an unforgettable and interesting night... in more ways than one. It was a lavish black tie do in Manchester, attended by a host of stars from the worlds of soap opera and football. Jean was not keen to travel far, and Peter stayed home to look after Daniel and Adam. Therefore, it was Natalia and her mum Marie who made the journey up north with myself and Bear.

The surprises began as soon as we arrived at the plush hotel. We weren't staying the night – Bear would have melted in a stuffy central-heated hotel – thus, I reserved a couple of rooms where we could freshen up and get into our glad-rags. I say 'us', meaning us humans; all Bear required was a quick brush and fluff up.

I think the ladies were looking forward to the glamour of the occasion. I, however, did not relish the prospect of being trussed up like a chicken. The last time I had been forced through etiquette to don a cardboard suit, it took forever to fasten the noose around my neck, and the unfamiliar restraints of the rest of the garment were, quite frankly, the most uncomfortable thing I had ever encountered. I would rather squash myself into a wet suit two sizes too small and stick on a waterproof name tag identifying myself as 'Quasimodo'.

The plan was that I would drive us all home to the Westcountry after the ceremony. This must have confused the staff, as people did not normally book rooms just for the day... well, not for our requirements anyway... if you get my drift. Unfortunately, due to this misunderstanding, they accidentally double-booked our rooms with certain people, who obviously had other things besides the grand event in store.

You can therefore imagine the hilarity of the events that unfolded after we arrived outside the first room. I slotted the key card into the lock, opened the door, and in we walked only to interrupt a couple rather enjoying their night away. The woman, an elegant lady in her seventies, with sculpted white hair and body draped in an expensive but somewhat dishevelled fashionable gown, shrieked and sprang back from her companion. I did not recognise the younger man in a black tie and little else, but I certainly recognised the lady, and so did Marie; it was the famous Katie Boyle.

Nowadays, many people would not be familiar with the (now late) actress and TV presenter who hosted the Eurovision Song Contest several times in the 1960s and 70s. For those that do not, Katie Boyle – also known as Lady Saunders – was the Amanda Holden and Davina McCall of her day. A few of us older folk may, however, remember her beautifully famous face, fronting the black and white adverts for 'Camay' – the soap laden with 'creamy moisturizer'.

Natalia, Marie, and I both stood there gawping. I suddenly found it extremely funny and resisted the urge to spout, 'I see you haven't forgotten the art of mustering a good lather-up then!' and just mumbled a garbled explanation. Bear, of course, stood there with his tongue hanging out because that's what Newfoundlands do – especially in stuffy hotels.

Thankfully, being as calm and sophisticated as a lady and her chauffeur could be, we all laughed it off. It could have been so much worse if Bear had not been there to break the ice.

"And who are you?" cooed Lady Saunders, approaching my drooling Newfoundland and making an enormous fuss over him.

"This is Bear," I mumbled.

"Oh, you're beautiful, aren't you? You are!" Ms Boyle smiled, completely taken with him.

Katie Boyle was a committee member of Battersea Dogs' Home and had also been invited to the awards event. We saw her later that night at the ceremony, acknowledging each other with a bashful wave.

It was a fantastic occasion. Bear won the award for Pet Dog of the Year, and it was a proud moment seeing my unassuming Newfie achieve a standing ovation from the likes of Sir Alex Ferguson, Bobby Charlton, and half the cast of Coronation Street. We bumped into William Roache later in the evening; he was extremely complimentary.

Not all the celebrity attention was welcome, though. Natalia was sixteen at the time and attracting a lot of admiring glances, looking beautiful and exquisite in her gorgeous red dress. A mature woman sporting a massive hairdo, gold earrings, and overly accentuated arched eyebrows sashayed over and gave us the briefest of congratulations before turning to Natalia and flashing a crimson lipstick smile.

"Darling," she drooled, in a broad southeast accent, pressing a business card into the teenager's hand. "If you're ever in London and looking for work, give me a call," before promptly swanning off into the crowd without elaborating.

Natalia was flattered, if not a little bewildered, whilst Marie looked pleasantly surprised. We all assumed the woman was from a modelling agency – until celebrity couple Neil and Christine Hamilton sidled over.

"Do you know who that was?" hissed Neil, the former Tory MP who had swapped political sleaze for showbiz schmoozing.

I shrugged. "Not a clue. Model scout or something?"

"It's Cynthia Payne," blurted Christine, barely able to conceal her glee.

Disappointed by our blank looks, Neil added: "Madam Cyn. You know?" He nudged me with his elbow. "The lady with the luncheon vouchers?"

Then I twigged. Cynthia Payne had been a notorious brothel keeper in the 1970s and 80s. She catered for a well-to-do clientele at her London home, where politicians, solicitors, and even vicars famously exchanged meal vouchers for her ladies' services.

Despite the scandalous headlines at the time, she had become a sort of 'naughty but nice' superstar over the years and a popular after-dinner speaker. That certainly accounted for her 'unusual persona'; in fact, in retrospect, I am surprised she was not selling raffle tickets. Marie, however, was not impressed and looked like she was about to punch Madam Cyn on the nose for trying to solicit the services of her daughter!

What a night it turned out to be – we all enjoyed the evening, especially Marie, who, let us say, partook of the alcoholic beverage a little too much; what a roller coaster of emotions was felt that evening! Probably, the only one of us who did not see what all the fuss was about was Bear, who simply sat patiently at my side until it was time to go home.

That was Bear, patient, polite, and a gentleman through and through.

These Newfies were the role models presented to Whizz when he moved in with us. From Izzie and Bear, he learned that he could belong; from Izzie and Bear, he learned that life could be an adventure, and from Izzie and Bear, he learned that he had massive pawprints to fill.

Natalie with Bear and David at the dog awards Manchester

Chapter Six: Bang, Crash, Splash!

I knew Whizz had settled in with everyone and everything the first time I caught him drinking from the downstairs loo.

"Oi! Get out of it," I said, nudging him out of Jean's ensuite into the bedroom where Bear and Izzie just happened to be 'inconspicuous' lookouts.

Whizz gave Izzie a look as if to say, 'We're busted guys – I told you we'd get caught!' but were his canine conspirators bothered? Not a jot! Bear did not bat an eyelid, an ear, or anything else, and Izzie just plodded off into the kitchen and slurped some fresh water from his drinking stand, of course, to prove that he had perfect manners and would NEVER drink out of a toilet. I stifled a chuckle, secretly pleased by this mini canine teamwork.

As the weeks passed by, there were other clues indicating the boys were bonding. I would wake up in the morning to find them all lying in a black and white heap at the bottom of my bed or find them gallivanting around the garden, Whizz pausing to cock a leg over my less-than-prized flower-pots again. Cheeky!

Huge shaggy dogs do not think much of central heating; even in midwinter, we were constantly nagged to open the door to the courtyard for a cooling off. To make life a whole lot easier, I put my joinery skills into action and designed a Newfie-sized 'cat-flap' with saloon doors, allowing access to some fresh air. It was actually more like a horse flap. The Lone Ranger and Tonto would not have been prouder at this marvelous feat of engineering.

Come dinner time; you would hear the crash bang as the three amigos charged into the bar. It was pointless me standing there like John Wayne chastising the inconsiderate entrance; finesse is not the forte of Newfoundlands, and if they want to push past you, they will. 'It's my house, and you are here for my convenience' seems to be their motto.

With our daughter far away at university, it was good to have the house full of larger-than-life characters and see Whizz grow from a nervous recluse into a confident member of the gang. He clearly could not believe his luck that he now had cuddles on tap and the freedom to roam freely in a house and garden – his house and garden.

As Whizz learned to trust us, devotion poured out of him like fizzy pop. He was unstoppable, a big ball of energy pinging around the house, squeezing through Bear's legs or clambering over a snoozing Izzie to be the first inside for dinner or the first outside for a walk.

Unlike bulky Bear and ageing Izzie with his dodgy windpipe, Whizz was light on his feet and not a heavy breather; you couldn't always hear him coming. He had this habit of padding stealthily up behind me and then sniffing my neck like Hannibal Lecter, making me jump out of my skin. More would fool me if I had a mug of tea in my hands!

It was hard work at times. Whizz was already a teenager in dog years, yet he had missed out on so much as a puppy. Having spent most of his first year of life alone in the shed, he craved attention and connection. Whether it was because I had been the one who had brought him home, I do not know, but he particularly wanted to be near me. I mean, really near, ideally eyeball to eyeball, nose to nose, and all the rest; visits to the bathroom were becoming downright awkward!

"Oof!" I would exclaim as he jumped up and planted his muddy paws on my shoulders. "Down, Whizz."

After everything he had been through, I could understand these bear hugs, but they had to stop. Jumping up was a no-no, especially with a disabled person in the house. Jean wore her mobile phone around her neck while I was out at work in order that she could call for help if she fell. You can imagine what it was like having three huge trip hazards in the house, especially those that liked to jump up or lie across doorways like snoring draught excluders. As for Whizz, he thought it was brilliant when one of us fell flat on our face as it made it much easier to say hello and have a slobbery face-to-face chat.

"I know you can get dogs for the disabled," groaned Jean one day after tripping over Whizz and being licked like a living lollipop. "But we've ended up with disabling dogs!"

Because Whizz had entered adolescence without being properly trained or socialised, I had to start from scratch with all the basic commands before moving on to impulse control. I thought it would be tough-going, but luckily, Whizz loved his food and learned fast through rewards and lots and lots of reassurance.

It was more than that, though; Whizz was always ready. He would lock eyes with me and cock his head to one side as if hanging on to my every word, then would go for it. He was earnest and eager to please. Every dog owner likes to project human feelings onto their pet; I get that. All I can say is it was a breeze to train Whizz how to fit into our household, and I cannot help thinking it was because he latched onto the idea that he had a second chance, and he did not want to blow it. Someone believed in him. I believed in him.

I was a bit of a rascal when I was a youth. Dad was strict, but his trade union commitments took him away most weekends. Sadly, unlike the other fathers, he never came to watch me play football or cricket for the school. I would have loved his support, but it was not to be. Mum turned a blind eye to my teenage scrapes, at least those of which she was vaguely suspicious. Actually – she did not know the half of it! As it was with most kids growing up in the sixties, I was out first thing after breakfast and back home just in time for tea.

A railway line ran through our east Bristol neighborhood (a cycle path now), and we used to play havoc there. The signalman befriended us and sent us on errands to fetch him bottles of lemonade from the off licence because he wasn't allowed to leave his post. One day, when he'd nipped to the toilet, we pilfered a couple of detonators from the signal box.

Little yellow capsules packed with explosives, they looked like sweets or pocket toys, but when you strapped one to the top of a rail, and a train wheel ran over it, there was an enormous bang. Signallers used them to warn drivers that there was heavy fog or a broken-down train up ahead, but we exploded them just for the fun of it. In those days, the railway police in their flower-pot hats used to patrol the tracks on Velocette motorbikes – silky quiet, they were. You would not hear a thing until they were almost on you; then, we would scatter in all directions. Miraculously, I never got caught. My mum would have let me get away with it, but my dad would have killed me!

The poet Lord Byron famously had a Newfoundland dog called Boatswain, who was a notorious troublemaker. He was always escaping and terrorizing the neighborhood, fighting other dogs and sowing his wild oats. In comparison, our Newfies were pretty tame as teenagers. Izzie was a bit of a handful back in the day, but the naughtiest thing Bear ever did was chew the zips off wetsuit boots.

Whizz was no rebel with paws, but as he grew bigger, stronger, and more confident, his excitement landed him in occasional trouble. He had a thing about horses and would bark like crazy whenever they passed the house on their regular treks along the bridlepath. One day, a neighbor turned up at our door with a very bewildered and sheepish Whizz by her side, tail between his legs. It turns out he had managed to leap over our five-bar gate into the lane and follow a horse and rider to the pub. Once he got there, though, he was not sure what to do with himself – (well, he could hardly order a pint, could he?) – and was very relieved when the landlady recognised him and brought him home.

I raised the height of the gate pretty smartish after that incident, but it did get me thinking. If Whizz had the guts and agility to leap over a five-bar gate like that, maybe he would have the guts and agility to leap off a moving boat.

I didn't have long to find out. In March, the new season began for Newfound Friends, and we returned to the training lake in the Cotswolds. As was the routine, we kept the dogs in separate vans until it was their turn in the water but left the rear doors open with the grille closed so they could breathe in plenty of fresh air and see what was going on outside.

Firstly, I let Whizz witness Izzie, Bear, and the others enjoying themselves, then led him down to the lakeside. Just like on the day we met, he hesitated at the edge, backing off when the lapping waters touched his paws. That did not bode well, but this time, as I started wading out, it was as if something clicked, and suddenly, he was right behind me. I crouched in the shallows and let him get used to the water swirling around his fur, supporting his weight.

"Alright, Whizz?" I murmured, patting his head. "You're alright."

During the mid-1990s, the base at nearby Fairford was used for the American B52 aircraft for bombing raids on Bosnia. The rumbling giants of these enormous aircraft would fly back and forth through the skies, casting a huge shadow plunging the training lake into the shade. Skimming very close to the surface of the lake, the stench of aviation fuel frightened the dogs, so we had to be wary, especially with a 'new Newfie' like Whizz.

I did not want to rush him. Memories of bad times in the water never leave you, and animals are no different from humans in that sense. I remember, when I was three or four, I nearly drowned. It all happened in an old flooded clay pit named the 'Lido' – it was situated in a part of Bristol called 'Fishponds.' Whether that was why it was called Fishponds, I do not really know. Maybe it was after the Lido, or maybe the Lido was named after Fishponds, which is a bit like the chicken and the egg!

It was very popular at the time. Mum used to take me as a tiny tot. Only the big boys swam in the quarry itself, as there was a smaller man-made pool for the kids. This particular day, I wandered in at the shallow end and just started walking. I still remember the moment when I was suddenly out of my depth and the gut-wrenching panic as my toes reached for the ground that disappeared beneath me. It must have been seconds, but it felt like hours until an arm came down and yanked me out; Mum, my saviour. That moment of sheer terror has never left my mind. After that incident, my dad insisted, 'he's got to learn to swim!' and signed me up for lessons at the local swimming baths. I have respected water ever since.

Whizz seemed relaxed in the shallows. I broke away from him and swam a short distance out into the lake, maybe twenty feet or so, thinking I would try to coax him into deeper waters. If he did not come, that would be okay; it was worth a try. To my delight, however, when I turned around, there he was, right behind me. We bumped noses, and he gave my face a huge lick.

"Ha! Well done, Whizz!" I laughed. "We'll make a water rescue dog of you yet."

I am a firm believer in quitting while you are ahead with dog training sessions. Better to end on a high, then the dog goes home remembering its success, not the challenge too far. For this reason, I did not push Whizz any further that day.

At the end of each session, we usually turn all the dogs loose into the lake and let them play. In my humble opinion, everyone should witness, at least once in their life, the sight of a dozen giant dogs having a pool party. Bring on the beer!

– Well, at least a few bowls of fresh water and some doggie treats. Remembering Whizz's bad experiences as a puppy, I wondered if he would growl at the other Newfies or shy away from them, but living with Izzie and Bear must have restored his faith in other dogs because he was more than happy to splash around with the others.

Over the following weeks, Whizz's confidence went stratospheric. By the end of his second training session, he was already jumping off a moving boat – I could not believe it! Some Newfies will never jump off a boat, come hell or high water, and certainly not one moving at speed, but Whizz seemed to relish it from day one. His tail would wag with delight as the cool blasts of wind whipped up his hair. He looked straight out of an exotic shampoo advert.

It was not just at the training lake that this new confidence showed. On dog walks, Whizz started seeking out any water he could find and jumping straight in. Back home, he would barge into Jean's bedroom and luxuriate in drying himself off by rolling around on her bed until the covers and pillows were completely soaked. I don't think it really frustrated Jean, especially after I flattered her, saying how much she loved washing and how good she was at it!

Six months after Whizz came to live with us, Newfound Friends was invited to take part in a festival to mark the two hundredth anniversary of the Battle of Trafalgar. The Royal Naval Dockyard in Portsmouth hosted the weekend of spectacular commemorations in June, and we were asked to come along and showcase the dog's life-saving skills.

Izzie's swimming days were over due to his breathing difficulties, and Whizz was only just starting out, so it was Bear I chose to bring with me to the three-day event. Swimming was not Bear's forte as his long legs often got a bit tangled, but he did us proud that weekend, which was lucky because we were being watched by massive crowds and filmed for Blue Peter.

The night before our final display, I rang Jean from our campsite just outside Portsmouth to check all was well. I had not anticipated Whizz's negative response to our absence.

"We're okay, but Whizz is being a real nuisance," she sighed. "He's been whining and off his food, barking his head off at horses and getting under my feet and all sorts. I think he's wondering where you are."

With some reluctance, I decided to travel back home and try to settle Whizz before heading back to Portsmouth in the early hours. However, when Bear and I went to set off the next morning, Whizz squeezed past us in the hallway and began patrolling the front door like an overzealous nightclub bouncer.

"It's alright, Whizz," I soothed. "We'll be back later. I promise."

Whizz was not convinced, though, and as I tried to nudge him back into the lounge while reaching for the door, he took desperate measures, jumping up and plonking his paws on my shoulders. 'There's no way I am letting you out the door without me!'

I looked at him. He looked at me with those doleful caramel eyes and twitching eyebrows. 'Well, this is embarrassing', he seemed to say. 'Yes, I do realize you've trained me not to do this, Dave, but you have left me no choice'.

I know I should have ordered him to get down immediately; there was something so endearing about those deep eyes looking into my soul that melted the command into mush – I just wanted to hug him. "Oh, alright," I sighed, giving in first. "Come on then, you silly spanner. Get down, and you can come with us."

Whizz let out a sort of gurgled bark, which I took to mean 'Good boy, Dave'.

When we arrived back at the Royal Naval Dockyard in Portsmouth, I managed to persuade one of my good friends, Keith, to supervise Whizz while Bear and I did our bit of the display. Keith was the commander of the Swansea unit of the Maritime Volunteer Service, a brilliant organisation whose skilled volunteers help out at maritime events and are trained to respond to emergencies at sea. The MVS Swansea guys were big friends of our charity and provided safety cover at many of our events in their rescue boat.

Well, that day, Keith was my lifesaver, taking Whizz off my hands to watch the display from the side-lines in the MVS rescue boat. Unfortunately, I do not think Whizz knew the meaning of sitting still in a moving boat. When he saw Bear and I leap into the water and start rescuing our 'casualty', he instantly decided he was definitely not going to miss out on the action. 'If you think I came all this way to sit in a boat, you are madly mistaken – I'm here! I'm here! Wait for me!'

Keith's crew tried to hold him back, but it was not easy to contain twelve stones of wriggling Newfie, and he soon slithered out of their clutches and hurtled into the water, landing with an almighty splash.

The MVS guys hardly dared look, but I burst out laughing when I saw Whizz swimming towards us, his giant black head bobbing along in the water.

"You mad banana," I groaned as he gate-crashed our display and escorted us all back to the Newfound Friends boat. My friends, Mark and Debbie, were in fits of giggles as they leaned out of the craft to heave us onboard.

"Got room for one more?" I grinned.

Once safely in the boat, Whizz did an ecstatic, giddy spin and put his paw on my arm as if to say, 'We make quite a team, don't we?'

We probably confused the thousands of people watching from the quayside, but Whizz was very pleased with himself, and I couldn't help but be pleased for him. He had just performed at the largest maritime festival ever held in the UK – not a bad way to make his debut, even if it was slightly unrehearsed.

Back home, there was no time to rest. The Blue Peter team was keen to get more Newfound Friends footage for their feature program on the Trafalgar bicentenary. It was always a pleasure to work with their producer Alex Leger, a gutsy and resourceful ex-army man. During his thirty years on the iconic children's TV program, he had been there, done that, and got every T-shirt going, from erupting volcanoes to warzone landmines, via tribes, tombs, and tapeworm. He was also a lovely person who listened to our ideas and would never surround himself with a big entourage when he could stick a camera on his shoulder and do the job himself.

After a day filming Bear and presenter Zoe Salmon in action on our training lake, Alex was keen to shoot some footage in the open sea, so I suggested we headed to Swansea, about ninety minutes' drive away. I have family roots in this beautiful part of South Wales, and Newfound Friends often trained there. It has a fantastic coastline where dogs are made very welcome. What's more, we could meet up with Keith and the rest of the Swansea Maritime Volunteer Service guys to provide safety cover for us while we filmed.

I arranged for one of our team members, Gordon, to come along and be 'rescued' by his dog Tess, a young black beauty who was one of our most experienced and skilled Newfies. I also needed a stand-in just in case Tess wasn't up for it on the day. Bear was knackered, so I decided to give Whizz his first-ever adventure in the open sea.

It was a roasting summer's day when we were locked out of Swansea marina. There were four rigid inflatable boats in our convoy, and after puttering into open waters, everyone opened their engines to top speed. I thought Whizz might be fazed by the sudden rush of wind billowing his fur and flapping his ears, but he stood calmly by my side, admiring the view as we bounced over the waves. I wondered how the young presenter, Zoe, would manage. A qualified lawyer and beauty queen (the former Miss Northern Ireland no less) with golden hair and dazzling teeth, she had only just joined the Blue Peter team and was already psyching herself up to jump into the chilly waters of the Bristol Channel.

Once we were a mile or so out, the underwater cameraman moved into position below the waves, and we were all set. Gordon jumped in and flailed about, pretending to be drowning while our boat circled him. On my signal, Zoe jumped off the moving boat clutching a torpedo life buoy, and Tess leapt in after her, performing a textbook rescue. What a pro! After one more take, the underwater cameraman gave the thumbs up to show he'd got everything he needed. Tess had delivered, Whizz could be stood down, and we could all go home.

Except that was not Whizz's idea of a fun day out. When he cottoned on that his services would not be required, he began straining at his lead and hollering in agitation, almost dragging me out of the boat. No way was he going to be left out of this one! There was no option but to let him have his jump with Zoe.

That was fine by us, but the poor presenter was starting to get the shivers.

"It's freezing!" she laughed through gritted teeth after being forced to jump into the sea for the third time.

At last, all that remained was for Zoe to do a short interview with me. She perched on the inflated edge of the boat while I sat opposite, one arm gripping Whizz.

"I said I would try anything once, and it's just been so much fun!" gushed the presenter just as Whizz leaned in to give her an affectionate nuzzle. Zoe giggled nervously and tried to dodge his big wet nose, but the move unbalanced her, and she slid backwards into the sea again, landing with a splash.

Whizz put his paw on the edge of the boat and gazed down at her in the water. "What are you doing down there, Zoe? Don't worry; I'll save you!" Whizz was clearly never going to sit on the side-lines or play stand-in for any other Newfoundland dog.

Not long after we hauled Zoe and Whizz back into the boat, Keith asked the Blue Peter presenter if she was alright, and she completely blanked him. Some people would have been offended, but for experienced seafarer Keith it was a red flag.

"Right, listen, guys," snapped the MVS commander. "We've got to get Zoe back quickly and get her warmed up. I think she's becoming hypothermic."

We all stared at the young woman. Keith was right. Even though it was still a hot day, Zoe's lips were blue and her face pale and passive. We wrapped her in foil blankets and made a dash back to Swansea marina.

Thanks to Keith we caught it in time, but only after a warm shower and a hot drink at the yacht club did the colour return to Zoe's cheeks. With it came her good humour, and she even handed out Blue Peter badges all round.

"Do I get a gold badge?" piped up Keith.

Zoe laughed awkwardly. "Er, sorry, no. We only give out gold badges for exceptional achievements, like..."

"Does saving your life count?" interrupted to Keith with a wink.

I am relieved to say that Zoe went on to host Blue Peter for another three years; her baptism of saltwater, obviously, did not put her off. As for Whizz, I was proud of him, he had not exactly been the water rescue hero of the day, but at least he had certainly made an impression! I did not know then that he was going to make up for it many times over.

Blue Peter presenter Zoe Salmon with David and Whizz

Chapter Seven: Newfound Friends

Whizz's adventures of becoming renowned as the World's best life-saving dog began eighteen years prior to his arrival at Days Cottage...

Jean and I set up Newfound Friends in 1989, two years after we bought our first ever Newfoundland dog, Thomas. Why a Newfoundland, you ask, rather than the smaller (well, slightly smaller) breeds we were used to?

Dogs have always featured in both our lives from the word go. My father trained our canine companions for film and TV in between his trade union commitments. The house was never without a German shepherd or boisterous Border collie.

Jean had a crossbred dog called Meg, a mixture of all sorts that she loved and comforted her through her childhood. Having been diagnosed with rheumatoid arthritis at the age of six and more or less isolated in hospital for two years, Meg became her best friend and soulmate. Thankfully, due to the expertise of rheumatologist Doctor Andrews, Jean was eventually able to return home, albeit in a wheelchair. Her illness has unfortunately blighted her ever since.

I met Jean when we were sixteen, and two years later, shortly after Meg passed away, Jade, a gorgeous German Shepherd, became our first 'jointly' owned pet, initially living with Jean until we married when we were twenty-one.

As lovely as he was, Jade's behavior left a lot to be desired. In fact, you would go so far as to say he could be downright naughty and frequently suffered from 'selective hearing'.

This was evidently apparent on our numerous walks around Ashton Park, a marvelous estate a short drive away from Jean's house on the outskirts of Bristol. Here you could walk for miles, and Jade was always away in his element, romping around, tossing the fresh cut grass or charging into piles of autumn leaves, scattering them aimlessly through the air, disturbing their peaceful graves. Of course, the recall was embarrassingly non-existent, but on the up, our acting careers were booming as we nonchalantly tootled along, pretending that his insane frolicking was all in the plan and everything was in complete control.

To be fair, he did not ever go far, and to his saving grace, there was one incident where we lost the van keys on one of our treks. On retracing our steps, Jade went bulldozing off, as usual, only to forage in the undergrowth and toss the wayward bunch high into the air like mother tossing pancakes.

That, I suppose, was his only claim to fame, but despite his crazy nature, he truly became our family friend, living to the ripe old age of twelve, departing from this earth around the time of the birth of our daughter Colleen.

It was not great being 'dogless', so our second German Shepherd, 'Kerry', joined our family, quickly forming and inseparable bond with Colleen. However, despite the good and friendly nature of Kerry, who you would trust with any adult or child, was blotted by the introduction of the dangerous dogs' act of the 1980s, and the reputation of such breeds was damming. Friends seemed to alienate Colleen, and reluctance to visit our house became all too apparent.

Once Kerry had passed on, we decided to look at other breeds. We had admired a large black Newfoundland that would sit beside the gate at the local pub. He was friendly and loved all the fuss bestowed upon him by passers-by; could we accommodate such a massive animal? – We also wanted to give a rescue dog a home... how did we choose? We did not – we did both.

Hence, we ended up contacting the Bath Cats and Dogs home and fell in love with a four-year-old Border Collie called Dylan (who incidentally should have been called

Houdini, the number of times we caught him flirting around with two lady Golden Retrievers in the village!)

Next to think big; really big! Thus, in 1987, the solid black huge Newfoundland pup came barging into our sedate family of Jean, Colleen, and myself and nudged us in a new direction. Thomas was a black Newfoundland purchased from a breeder named Lucy Stephenson. Lucy lived in a small cottage situated in the Devon countryside. The cottage was aptly named 'Little Silver'; however, despite the relatively insignificant size of the building, it was still packed with a hoard of extremely large dogs. It was to be the start of a long association.

I did not tell my wife and my daughter of Thomas's imminent arrival, and it was a heart-warming sight to see the look on their faces as I plonked the great black furball into Coleen's arms. Dylan also was pleasantly welcoming and the two bonded immediately. It must have come as a cruel blow to Thomas, as did us all when Dylan passed away from cancer shortly after.

We had been told that Newfoundlands were natural swimmers and that we should fence off any ponds (and even keep the loo seat down!), but at first, seeing no real signs of uncontrollable liquid fetish, we thought of Thomas as more of a pipe-and-slippers sort of dog. How wrong could you be

– everything changed a few months later when we took him on a short 'relaxing' break to the Scottish borders.

On arrival at our rented cottage near Peebles, I marvelled at the beautiful chocolate box dwelling, nestling in the quiet countryside; just the place for a few days away with Jean and our daughter Colleen, aged nine. 'This was the life!'

'Peace' did not last long. I barely opened the car door when Thomas flew out, bolting across two fields and disappearing out of sight.

"Thomas!' shrieked little Colleen. "Thomas! Thomas!"

I left Jean with our worried daughter and raced across the fields, praying that our placid pipe-and-slippers dog had not turned into a bloodthirsty lamb-and-bunny dog or, worse, run onto a busy road. As I crested the second field, I immediately calmed as I saw a majestic sight; the long, winding River Tweed – and there was Thomas up to his neck in it, swimming up and down and looking very pleased with himself. By the look on his face, totally oblivious to the panic he had caused, you could tell perfect paradise had been found.

After staggering down the bank and wading in, I finally managed to attach a lead to his soggy collar and guided him onto dry land. Thomas showed me what he thought of that by shaking his great coat and drenching me from head to toe.

The look on my family's faces as we walked towards them, soaking wet, leaving trails of river juice shining across the lush green grass, was priceless. – 'Swamp-thing' did not even come close.

How Thomas knew there was a river there and why he launched himself into the water with such confidence, I will never know. He had never swum before, but I guess it was his way of saying he wanted to be a water rescue dog just like his ancestors.

As soon as we got back to North Somerset, Jean and I began reading up on the history of the Newfoundland dog. It dates back to the sixteenth century when European fishermen began crossing the Atlantic in large numbers in search of cod. They took strong dogs with them to pull carts and haul in fishing nets and settled in both Labrador, a cultural region on the easternmost Canadian mainland, and Newfoundland, a large island (as big as Ireland) situated off the same coast.

Nobody knows exactly which breeds of dog the fishermen chose, but among them were probably the Portuguese water dog and the (now extinct) Great Rough water dog, both of which were good retrievers and had the peculiar trait of webbed feet, which facilitated excellent swimming skills.

It is not surprising that dogs with webbed feet were highly prized. Not only could the animals be trained to bring in the nets, but they could also retrieve objects that fell overboard – including the men themselves. Shipwrecks and drownings were not uncommon, and the dogs developed a heroic reputation for sensing when people were in trouble

Over time, a hardy black and white breed with a talent for retrieving and swimming emerged named the St-John's dog after the provincial capital. From this now extinct breed, some dogs were selectively bred for their salvaging skills and gradually developed into the Labrador Retriever so popular today.

Others were selectively bred for their large size, mighty lung capacity, and thick fur, which insulated them against the cold temperatures of the Atlantic. These animals became known as Newfoundlands – as they are still aptly named today.

One of their most impressive attributes is a double-layered coat, the outer layer of which has a water-resistant oily base. Air is trapped between the two layers, giving extra buoyancy and keeping them warm, just like a human's wetsuit. Even though this shaggy coat makes a Newfie less streamlined in the water than some dogs, its big tail compensates, adding a powerful rudder to enhance the unique action in the water. If you see them powering along, mastering the breaststroke with all four legs – a doggy four-wheel-drive will spring to mind. All in all, Newfoundlands are supremely cut out to be the 'St Bernard' super heroes of the sea.

As tales of the dogs' intelligence and derring-do qualities spread back to Europe, Newfoundlands became the ultimate faithful friends of well-to-do families and gentry; the cachet sometimes had tragic results. Dog-nappers targeted valuable animals, and many an owner fought to defend their beloved pets. In 1803, a colonel was killed in a duel by a distinguished naval captain after the two gentlemen got into a quarrel over their scrapping Newfies in London's Hyde Park. What a way to die!

Can you imagine that today – two old ladies fighting over a couple of Yorkshire Terriers in the local park? The worst that would probably happen (which, to be honest, is highly dangerous and likely to entice them to accompany the local PC to the station for a chat and a coffee) is a bash around the chest with a walking stick or a Greggs sausage roll chucked in a face.

Newfies, of course, are a lot stronger than Yorkshire Terriers, and papers of the eighteenth and nineteenth centuries are peppered with accounts of the brave dogs driving away robbers, rescuing people from burning buildings, and spontaneously diving into rivers and lakes to save hapless people and pets from a watery grave.

Napoleon Bonaparte himself owed his life to a fisherman's Newfoundland who kept the French emperor afloat when he got knocked into rough seas on a voyage home to France. Reputedly, in 1900, also in France, the police in Paris recruited a squad of Newfoundlands to drag people out of River Seine – with mixed results. According to a (possibly apocryphal) report, one of the trainee dogs was so thrilled with the juicy beefsteak he was given for rescuing a drowning child that he started pushing children into the river in order to rescue them!

Jean and I had more modest aspirations for our boy Thomas; however, realizing he was harking back to his ancestry, we channeled his talents and cast the net wide for someone who could teach him – and me – the art of water rescue.

The nearest group that showed any interest in us was 'Plymouth Sporting Newfoundlands', an association based in Devon whose founders, Tony Mayor and Tom Rudd, had an exceptional experience in water rescue work. As it turned out, the two-hundred-and-forty-mile round trip to visit them was worth every penny. Tony and Tom also had close ties with Terra Nova Sportive (TNS), a Paris-based group regarded as world leaders in Newfoundland water rescue training and more than willing to travel to the UK to exchange ideas and help us learn.

Thomas was still a puppy, but he'd had all his initial injections, and I already knew he was confident in the water; we were ready and willing; it was just a matter of learning the ropes.

Most of our training took place in fairly shallow waters off the south coast of Devon or neighboring Cornwall. Initially, I had to swim a few meters away from Thomas, then call him to swim towards me. As he approached, I had to tap the surface of the water to attract his attention, then gradually turn into a semi-circle, tapping the water along the way. The idea being, that Thomas learned to follow the splashes and ended up with his nose facing back to the shore. I was then to hold onto his harness, say 'shore', and get towed back to dry land, lying flat on my back.

The harnesses were specially made from soft pig's skin. Straps pass between the dog's front legs and link to another strap that goes round the dog's belly; these are duly secured with brass buckles. There are strong rubber rings for the casualty to grip and, to facilitate lifting the animal into the rescue boat, a strong stainless-steel handle stands tall. Three decades on, I still have these same harnesses, kept in good condition thanks to the odd repair by a local leather craftsman.

Thomas learned fast, faster than me anyway! He thrived on praise, and after vast amounts of repetition over a few weeks, he was ready to expand his repertoire to holding exercises. We threw floats with a rope attached into the water and asked Thomas to fetch them. He found this great fun, especially when the floats were large plastic bottles (with the lid removed), as these made a satisfying crunching noise when his jaws latched onto them.

Once our budding canine rescuer was used to holding objects, despite his young age, he was strong and quickly learned how to tow a rigid inflatable boat to shore, holding one end of a rope while I sat in the boat holding the other – (for safety reasons, we never attached the rope to the boat or any dogs; it's very important that they can let go and swim free of any encumbrance if they get into trouble). It is an amazing and unbelievable feeling sitting in a boat being towed by a puppy!

The next step in the program is moving on to working with life-saving rings. I had to play the casualty and put my arm through the lifebuoy; then, Thomas would grip the rope attached to it and pull me to shore. We also repeated the exercise with red plastic lifeguard's torpedoes – akin to those used in the TV show 'Baywatch'... though there the similarity with David Hasselhoff and Pamela Anderson ends... much too chilly for that attire!

It was all very invigorating, but my favorite part of the training was when Thomas and I learned to leap off a moving boat together and swim towards a 'casualty'. This is where the personality of your dog comes to the fore.

Some dogs will leap off the boat first time and soar ten feet through the air like Superman. Others will hang back up until they pluck up the courage and bellyflop into the water as close to the boat as possible. Some will never jump come hell or high water, and you have to respect that. Newfoundlands are the ultimate Stonewall Jacksons, and you cannot force them to do something they do not want to do. I have witnessed impatient owners ruin everything by chucking their anxious dogs into the water and wondering, after, why their poor, traumatized pet refuses to go anywhere near a boat again.

Fortunately, Thomas was up for it from day one. It was exhilarating, diving off a moving boat into the waves and hearing the splash as my enormous companion landed by my side. We would swim together towards the 'victim' and then practice the instructions – 'hold' and 'boat'; meaning that

Thomas was to swim close enough for the casualty to grip the harness, then return them both safely to the rescue boat.

During my time with Plymouth Sporting Newfoundlands, I learned a few crucial lessons, most of them the hard way. For starters, never swim with a Newfoundland on your own. It is just about impossible to pull a thirteen-stone dog out of the water and into a boat as it is, never mind when it's sopping wet and weighing a stone heavier.

The second most important thing – never expect your dog to swim in water that you are not ready and able to get in yourself. It sounds obvious, but if you are going to ask a dog to jump into the sea, it is essential that you are a proficient swimmer. You must also understand tides, currents, and the effects of all weather conditions.

There is also another reason why dog handlers have to be prepared to plunge into the water themselves. In a real-life rescue scenario, the one thing a dog is unable to do is talking to the casualty. A panic-stricken person at risk of drowning has immense strength and can drag even a Newfoundland under. The sight of an immense animal lunging towards a victim who is already terrified can be daunting, to say the least. It is therefore important that a human is there to reassure, calm the person down and explain what is going to happen.

Despite the amazing natural ability of the dogs, unfortunately, even the mighty Newfoundland dog can get into trouble, as I, unfortunately, found out whilst training one day with the Plymouth guys off a beach in Devon.

We were running a few drills when a family with Newfoundlands were inquisitive as to our activities of the day. Chatting confidently away, they told us how great their dogs were at swimming, waved goodbye, and moved further along the beach. A few minutes later, they came running back towards us, shouting for help.

Their dogs were good swimmers, alright – but they were not trained to come back to shore. Scanning the sea, we could just make out two tiny blobs on the horizon about to disappear from view. Thank goodness we had a couple of inflatable boats and the manpower to pull the dogs onboard; otherwise, they could have been lost forever or even caught in an ebbing tide, whisked across the channel, applied for French nationality, and changed their names to 'Les Chiens!'

To avoid such tragedies, Plymouth Sporting Newfoundlands encouraged all its members to join the Royal Life Saving Society, accomplish their life-saving qualifications, and obtain the Royal Yachting Association boat and skipper certifications. It is not just the dogs that need to be experts in their field – the lives of all depend on it!

My apprenticeship with the Plymouth guys lasted off and on for five years. In between the course, I was keen to put these newfound skills into action closer to home and pass on my valuable knowledge gained.

Although I live only a few minutes' drive from Portishead, situated directly on the coastal Bristol Channel, it would have been dangerous to train dogs in this area. The estuarine section of the River Severn, where it merges with the sea, is not only a busy shipping lane with treacherous mudflats; pipped to the post by Canada's Bay of Fundy, it has the second highest rise and fall of tidal waters in the world.

We were finding it difficult to decide on a suitable site, safe and as local as possible, when a friend suggested Cotswold Water Park. With its vast area of gravel quarries, naturally filled with water to create more than one hundred and seventy lakes, the place would be ideal.

Everybody seemed keen, apart from the park warden, who did not relish the thought of a dozen dogs muddying his crystal-clear gravel-filtered heaven. At the mention of 'charity', he relented and agreed we could put on a display of the dogs' skills in one of the lakes as a one-off event.

Therefore, with the help of a few friends, business contacts, and the boys from Plymouth, that is exactly what we did. The day was a great success and resulted in thousands of pounds being raised for CLIC (now CLIC Sargent), – a charity that provides accommodation on hospital grounds for families of children with cancer.

For Jean and me, it was a revelation. If we could raise money for a great cause just by inviting people to watch a bunch of big dogs splashing around, then why not make it a regular occurrence? As for the 'one-off event', thankfully, one of the quarry owners said we could use a lake of theirs for training on a regular basis; problem solved!

In the early days, Newfound Friends was not a registered charity. We were just a bunch of like-minded Newfie owners who met up to have fun, teach our dogs new tricks, and put on the odd fundraiser in aid of good causes. Jean adored the dogs and would have loved to have jumped in and joined in all the fun, but her disability meant she could not swim, and she was terrified of the water. Determined to play an active part, she took on the job of administrator, taking care of the legalities and paperwork.

Thankfully, my wife was still able to accompany and enjoy our outside activities and fulfilled the essential role of keeping a watchful eye on all the dogs left on dry land while we were out on the boat. One would be forgiven if this seemed to be a small task. A few large, but well-trained dogs, frolicking around at a charity event? How hard could it be?

Believe it or not, people will stop at nothing for monetary gain, and a non-profit, fund-raising event for a good cause is sad, no exception. We realized this on one such occasion, almost to our detriment, when we actually caught a man and woman walking off with one of the team's dogs. The brazen couple cobbled up some excuse about how they thought the dog needed a walk! They handed the dog back to us, but it was a hard lesson learnt, and we never left the dogs unsupervised again.

It was not only the dogs that needed surveillance. I remember one dreadful day at the training lake when Colleen and Thomas disappeared. I returned to the shore from a stint on the lake and immediately realized they were nowhere to be seen. My blood ran cold; Colleen was only around nine years of age, and despite the fact I had every faith in her protection by almighty Thomas, it suddenly dawned on me that anything could have happened.

It felt like a lifetime before someone from the team spotted the breakaway couple, half a mile away, on the far side of the water. We jumped in the van and drove round the lake to find them sitting on the bank in the sunshine, looking happy and relaxed. Unaware of any fuss they may have caused, the pair of little monkeys decided to have a nice swim together without telling anyone what they were up to. It seemed, ironically, the fundamentals of water safety had not been successfully drilled into her little brain – however, she certainly remembered them after that day!

It was a steep learning curve for all of us. As well as training up the dogs and team members, we had to buck up with safeguarding procedures. People were not just prepared to stand on the quayside and watch displays; they wanted to get in the water and be 'rescued' by the dogs!

We quickly clocked that this was a brilliant way to raise money, and it still is. Not only do charities benefit from all the sponsorship, but the participants also have an amazing and occasionally life-changing experience. Many of them are terrified of water; some cannot swim or have disabilities that affect their independence or confidence. A few are even scared of dogs! Yet, all get into the water and allow themselves to be towed to safety by a great hulking Newfoundland. Looking at the delight on their faces and admiring the hugs they give their canine 'rescuers'' after incredible heroism is a reward in itself, making the hours of extensive training thoroughly worthwhile.

Things really took off for Newfound Friends in 1995 when the Daily Telegraph published a story, written by their animal behavior journalist Celia Haddon, depicting the group and our cause. Tracey Morgan, our photographer, provided the shots and the overwhelming success of the publicity sent us all whirling. Over the following weeks, more than one thousand letters of support and admiration poured through our letterbox, arriving from all over the country and across the world.

We were well up the tree in the doggie world and reaching beyond the canopy. I was even approached by Radio four; briefly, I do believe my thick Bristolian accent put them off – too many 'ers and all-right me babbers' – they probably did not understand a word I said.

Despite this minor rebuff, TV crews began to arrive at our little cottage in North Somerset, and life was never the same again.

All action Whizz flying through the air at Plymouth Sound

Chapter Eight: Festivals and Heroes

Newfound friends were fast becoming in demand; festival and celebration invitations flooded in, even before Whizz arrived to top the bill and cement the icing on the cake. Things were moving fast, and we soon welcomed another Newfoundland, Harry, into our brood.

Bristol is famous for its maritime connections, steeped in seafaring history; it provides a perfect setting for many events and an excellent home base for the charity. One of the main annual celebrations is the huge Bristol Harbor Festival. I am proud to have been involved in this great occasion for the last twenty-five years or so, and hopefully, many more to come.

There were, of course, numerous others, giving opportunities for publicity and ultimately raising funds. I feel the most memorable was an occasion blessed with Royalty; we actually met the Queen... albeit in a fridge...

Local business man St John Hartnell, well-to-do and probably one who completes the Times crossword in five minutes, was the main principle and source behind the John Cabot five-hundred-year celebrations. He contacted us in 1995 to request our involvement, and ultimately, we became good friends, to the extent that St John became a great ambassador for our charity.

John Cabot was renowned for his oceanic expedition and, in particular, one journey on a ship named 'The Matthew'; he sailed from Bristol to Newfoundland in North America in the glorious year of 1497. To celebrate the event, a complete replica of the Matthew was built, and a whole re-enactment of the voyage took place in 1997. The Newfoundland heritage connection with the dogs was a perfect complement to the occasion, and Harry was to be The Matthew's mascot; how Whizz would have loved it!

The celebrations were massive, spaced over several days prior to the sail. I was asked to put on a display with the dogs, and due to the scale of the event, I commandeered the help of a few buddies. The Plymouth team were only too pleased to take part, and Mark Anderson, a good friend from Sheffield, also arrived with his dog, Bernie.

It was a great success, attended by very important people, including the patron, the (now sadly, late) Duke of Edinburgh, who I met on several occasions. His interest in charity was genuine and obvious. The dogs were so popular with all involved that each received honorary citizenship of Newfoundland Island, together with a prestigious gold medal.

The replica Matthew set sail on its trail to the discovery of the New Found Lands at the end of May 1997 to huge fanfare from the citizens of Bristol. The small wooden ship, with its oak panels and billowing sails, was almost dwarfed as it slipped under the iconic Clifton suspension Bridge and made its way out into the Bristol Channel. You would wonder how such a tiny vessel managed the four-week journey all those years ago, but I guess it was a tiny warrior of its time. That day, as I watched, I had a funny but probably inappropriate thought of how easy it would be to make a model with a couple of tubes of glue and a few boxes of Swan Vestas.

Thankfully, St John and the team were not destined to be swashbuckling pirates, and we arrived by charter flight to Saint John's, the capital of Newfoundland, then onward by car to Bonavista, a small coastal village, where John Cabot was reputed to have discovered New Found Lands. We arrived in plenty of time to greet the arrival of The Matthew, due to dock during the following day.

The island was small, dotted with a few pastel-colored, timber houses spread thinly amongst the mass of forest greenery. No Hilton luxury here, but the friendly villagers welcomed us all into their homes, a much preferred and lovely way to understand the native way of life.

Unfortunately, the weather was not so inviting; in fact, it was bloody freezing. It was mid-summer, but the huge icebergs still reigned threat over the harbor entrance. Goodness knows what it would have been like in the winter. I could see in earnest why the great Newfoundland dogs are such tough creatures.

A reigning threat in more ways than one, it turned out. No other than her Majesty the Queen, together with Prince Phillip, drew up in a shiny black limousine to the delight of the crowds as we all gathered to welcome the Matthew as it sailed through the perilous icy waters to its destination.

St. John confidently introduced the contingents from Bristol to the Queen and the Duke as they slowly negotiated the long line. I, of course, was near the end, trying to look composed and stop my teeth from chattering and my knobbly knees from nobbling. As they drew close, I heard Prince Phillip say to Her Majesty that I owned a Landseer Newfoundland dog. I was aware of her love of animals and her own Corgis but was still delighted in her true interest as she enquired about Harry's name.

I ventured to reply, "Harry and another one at home, Thomas."

Honored I was as she moved on to receive a Newfoundland Tartan and a nice warm blanket draped round her shoulders by Brian Tobin, the Premier of the province.

The celebrations continued long after the Royals left. Visitors came from as far as Seattle and Vancouver, gathering other Newfoundland owners along the way. It became known as the Great Newfoundland Dog Trek. St John invited them aboard for photographs with the cabin and crew. Despite the absence of Harry, who remained at home, it was a fantastic day I will never forget – even though I was freezing what's left of my nuts off.

The Matthew continued touring elsewhere, and after the east coast of Canada was navigated, it was time to come home to roost. I was pleasantly surprised to receive a letter from Buckingham Palace asking me to present a second, carefully folded, enclosed correspondence to David Alan Williams, the captain of the Matthew, upon its return. I wondered why the queen chose to send the letter to me, maybe it was the influence of St John or perhaps her love of dogs – who knows, but I felt privileged, to say the least.

At the time, we had two children from Belarus staying with us. Sasha Kotovich and Alan Sychesky (aged nine and ten) were receiving respite care and treatment from the effects of the nuclear Chernobyl disaster. (Their stories will be told later in the book.) What a delight it would be for those boys to present the letter themselves. Not speaking a word of English, I am not sure whether they were aware of the importance of it all, but they performed the task superbly; I am sure it uplifted their spirits.

With more invites to attend other Maritime events, the Newfound Friends team was rapidly expanding. Friends Mark and Sue from Swindon, Keith, Karina from Cheltenham, and Debbie and Tim from Bristol all joined the group, adding to our canine talents with their own Newfoundlands. It was in 1999 that we took part in the annual Shanty Event in Swansea.

Our long association was established with Swansea, and thus it was, ten years down the line, that we were asked to take part in the Cardiff Bay August bank holiday festival... and Whizz flew into his own.

Cardiff Bay was much changed from my boyhood visits to the Principality. The old coal docks are gone and replaced with swanky restaurants, shops, and apartments. The magnificent Welsh Assembly building completed the transformation leaving little parts of Tiger Bay alive to portray a brief insight into the area of multicultural past.

The actual bay now separates the river Taff from the Bristol channel via huge lock gates, turning the water into a kind of giant lake – superb for water sports!

The Newfoundland dog display, as always, was a great draw for the crowds who would line the banks of the bay. We became a firm favorite at Cardiff, making good friendships with the locals and the other participants of the festival. We were, however, also there for safety cover for other participants – the Royal artillery and Blackhawk parachute displays, amongst others.

Parachutists would descend from small planes, skillfully maneuvering with pulls and tugs to the ropes, landing upon a designated marker in the water. Newfound Friends had a good relationship with the Hawks, and we were always bobbing around safely in the distance, just in case things went wrong – which on this occasion, it sadly did.

The final attempt was made by a guy sporting a massive chute, brightly decorated with the Welsh Dragon Flag. Through no fault of his own, a sudden gust of wind caught the billowing parachute, ushing it away from the marker and tangling the cords unceremoniously around the fabric, incarcerating the poor chap, rendering him helpless.

Suffice it to say, Whizz was more than enthusiastic, sensing the danger as we set off at pace towards the

Blackhawk. I was driving at full pelt as Tim desperately tried to hold Whizz back, clinging on to his harness for dear life, whilst Keith scanned the scene, and assessing the situation as best he could.

"Not yet, Whizz!" Tim cried, to no avail, as the superhero leapt from the boat and flew through the air, landing in the water with an almighty splash and swimming strongly to the victim.

Thankfully, the soldier managed to release his straps and clear himself from the parachute. By the time we had reached him, Whizz was already doing his job, sidling right up to him.

"Grab his harness!" I shouted, "He will do the rest!"

Whizz was in his element and knew exactly what to do, swimming towards us, then circling until we could get them both back on board. Of course, Whizz welcomed the survivor by soaking him even more as he shook his shaggy coat free of the water. Evidently grateful, the Blackhawk thanked Whizz for the shower and gave him a massive cuddle.

Keith jumped into the drink to gather up the parachute, keeping it well away from our craft whilst he dealt with the flailing ropes to avoid loss of the expensive equipment and, more importantly, to ensure no damage to ours or any other boats.

We arrived back to shore, greeted by rapturous applause by the thousands of festival-goers lined along the quay... most of us, that is. The Blackhawk received a bit of jip, but to be fair, a gust of wind is, well, a gust of wind!

The commentator, also in his element, I might add, made an appeal for the volunteers to hold the dogs. No shortage there – even though everyone involved suffered a soaking, fun was had by all... and a real rescue! What more could they want?

Whizz was the hero of the day and much fuss he had too.... not that he was at all bothered; for him, it was just another day at the office. We just had to keep him away from Boswell, another large Newfoundland, or a scrap would surely ensue. Suffice it to say, Blackhawks and Newfound Friends from that day developed a great bonding.

This, however, was not quite the end of the day. Whizz was already super excited, and it took two very strong Welsh rugby players to hold on to my boy. He was not finished yet! I am sure he would have done the whole show on his own if we had let him!

To finish the displays, we always ended with a re-enactment of the Swansea Jack rescue of puppies – in honor of 'Jack' who amazingly dived into the North Swansea Docks, retrieving a hessian sack full of a litter of tiny babies.

Obviously, we do not use puppies, but a cuddly toy dog, which, after its timely rescue, is presented to a chosen child from the audience, along with the opportunity for photos, with the parents and Whizz, who had jumped majestically from the pontoon and completed this wonderful task.

As with any big event, the mopping up is the worst and takes absolutely forever. The crowds hovering, wanting photos, and cuddling with the dogs, are welcoming but literally go on and on. We patiently wait until the bulk disappears before we attempt to retrieve our equipment and make our way home.

On this particular occasion, whilst we were hanging around, I became involved in a brief conversation with a gentleman who was connected to the History TV channel and was interested in making a film. We made tentative arrangements to discuss it all the following week... amazing what contacts you make at these events... one thing often leads to another, or so I thought.

Collecting our boat entailed travelling through a restricted area to the only slipway in the Bay that facilitated a launch for our small craft. It was not used that much, but such a simple job to slide the trailer down the algae-covered concrete in anticipation of the arrival of Keith with the inflatable.

No, it was far from a simple job – yours truly slipped on the green goo, and flat on my back, sloshed along the soggy mess to the water's edge.

You try to be brave as your colleagues help you up, but it was agony driving back through the traffic to North Somerset, and I was cursing every family that ventured out that day with their sodding cheese sandwiches and cans of coke. 'Never mind', I said to myself... 'don't moan; it's all for a good cause, and where would we be without the fabulous public!'

The accident took my mind back to a few years ago when I had to re-position a staircase in a large office block overlooking Bristol harbor side. The job had to be finished before a power boat race that was due to start in the afternoon. I was confident I could manage... I remember the pain in my legs as the stairs slipped and crashed to the ground pinning my 'pins' to the floor. How I got out of the building, I will never know; my lower limbs swelled up larger than a bloated Michelin man.

Back home, after the Cardiff festival, the 'boys', with their endless energy, looked at me eagerly for a walk. No chance of that; it was meals for all, a hot shower for me, and off to bed.

I was in a fair bit of discomfort and had to take a few days off work. As I was recuperating, I received a call from the young man I had met at the festival to discuss the impending film for the History Channel. His intention was for one of our dogs to be part of a program that explained how livestock was transported in the Middle Ages. Seemed like a good idea at the time.

Their original plan was to use a donkey on a raft floating down a tranquil river... hmm. His concern was a donkey was probably at risk of drowning and imminent death, and one of our dogs could substitute as that would be safer. I knew Whizz would not really fit the bill as he would be off in a shot from the raft into the river for a nice leisurely swim. I felt Bailey, Debbie's large Brown Newfoundland, would be an excellent choice as he was huge, placid, and, more importantly, was not obsessed with swimming in every pool on earth.

Plans were made, and a date was set for a few weeks' time on a Saturday in mid-September. The impending day arrived, and I was ready to leave for this momentous occasion. Whizz was, as usual, disappointed at being left behind, gave me his knowing look; 'how about me?'

"Not today, Whizz your turn tomorrow." – training at our lake in Gloucestershire.

I picked up Debbie from Bristol, and we arrived at the meeting point high up in the Brecon beacons. Greeted by a researcher from the TV production company, we followed her down a narrow footpath to a grassy, remote location on the banks of the fully flooded River Wye.

We could not really believe what stood before us. The 'raft', if you could call it that, was no more than a few planks of driftwood loosely tied together with a few strands of thin string; it was ricketier than my grandma's arthritic legs. A good job Whizz was not with us, or he would have jumped upon it and smashed it to bits; then, on second thoughts, he probably would have saved another life by destroying the mess before anyone got hurt.

It was an easy, instant decision for us both to say our goodbyes and make our way back home. There was no way we would put one of our dogs in that kind of danger, so that ended any chance of fame and fortune for Bailey – at least on TV!

Returning to our house, Whizz bounded towards me, elated that I had not been gone that long after all. I looked into his huge soppy eyes and gave him an almighty cuddle.

"Well, Whizz, you did not miss a thing – it was definitely not one for you this time!"

Whizz to a spectacular rescue at the Cardiff Bay festival

Chapter Nine: Swansea

Our association with Swansea bloomed, and it became one of our favorite places in South Wales to be. It was perfect in many ways and in an ideal geographical position, being only an hour from our home in North Somerset.

Whizz was an astute dog with senses and intelligence that set him apart from his canine friends. He was able to suss out what was going on with all and sundry – sometimes even before us! Swansea was no exception, and as soon as we hit The Prince of Wales Bridge, he would sniff the sea air, wag his tail, and bark with delight, the verbal outburst increasing in volume as we neared the city. He just could not wait to see all his friends. We loved to see Whizz happy, and we never doused his wonderful spirits, but now and again, the old 'ear oles' became ever so slightly overwhelmed!

This weekend was a little different, as it was the Mumbles Navy Day organized by our good friend, Swansea councilor Antony Colburn. The Mumbles is a popular bay situated towards the western end of Swansea, and Navy Day takes place on the third Saturday in June each year.

Whizz's celebrity status was rapidly expanding, and media interest was growing. Therefore, it was, as well as the participation in the Navy Day celebration, we were asked to film with the BBC, for their *Country File* program on a Sunday – It was to be a busy weekend... but that's how it is when you are a star.

Whizz and I arranged to stay overnight with my Auntie Mary at her home in Bishopston, just north of the Mumbles. Whizz loved my aunt, as she always made such a fuss of him. Of course, the hearty treats of Swansea market, minced prime steak laden with lush beef gravy, had nothing to do with it whatsoever – much more enticing after a day out at sea than healthy cooked chicken and Pro Plan complete!

Antony Colburn was also a very special friend of Whizz, and his council connections opened so many doors, enabling Whizz to work on the beaches and bays in the area. He single-handedly organized the Mumbles Navy days and was always the first to greet the whole team of Newfound Friends when we arrived at the Mumbles promenade.

The event was immensely popular, and this year was no exception. As the dogs stretched their legs after the drive to South Wales, the crowds soon gathered; you could not walk far without someone stopping for a bit of a chat and a lot of fuss.

Gordon towed our boat over from our base in the Cotswolds, and we all waited on the slipway to help prepare it for launch. The timing was essential, the tide was just about coming in, and this Swansea Bay high water gave us a window of around an hour before the sea retreated, which would make a recovery difficult.

As we prepared to put the boat into the water, the BBC producer of *Country File* appeared and asked if he could film the Saturday display as it might be useful for the program. This was a brilliant idea, as each and every dog has a chance in a display to show off their individual skills. Some of our dogs are good at one particular exercise, others like Whizz are adept at all. Fairness is key in showmanship and education; the dogs only learn by osmosis if they are given a chance to observe their colleagues, develop their talents and relish in their own success.

The day was a triumph; the large numbers of people massed along the Promenade, clapping and cheering all the dogs in turn. Antony, knowing every animal by name, watched each one, bellowing out encouragement as they strove to complete their tasks. It was the icing on a magnificent cake when the BBC filmed a little of Antony's Navy Day and broadcasted the footage a few weeks later.

As the show came to an end, the BBC producer tried to pull me aside to talk a little more about the *Country File* film taking place the following day. I had to explain that we needed to get the boat out of the water very quickly as the tide was going out. Thankfully, he patiently waited while it was secured on the trailer and towed onto dry land before we continued the conversation.

It had been a long day already, and I was grateful that most of the discussions and arrangements regarding the production had been cemented a month or so prior to the actual filming.

The researchers had already asked for advice concerning the best location to film the action, together with possible procedure and content. They learned that the dogs thrive best, working in their natural environment – the open sea – and that we had previously filmed the dogs with the Blue Peter team out in the wilds of the Bristol Channel. The head of the production had also spoken to me as to the best way to capture the activities, and a viewing of the Blue Peter episode was invaluable to all.

As it happened, it was the producer's first assignment with the BBC, and even though it extended an already long tiring day, I was very happy to bestow my massive (!) box of expertise upon his brain... Not sure about Whizz, who, as usual, literally poked his nose into every word exchanged.

I had also suggested during the weeks before that we feature Swansea Jack, the legionary rescue dog from the town, as he always featured in our displays, and you could hardly leave him out. I was pleasantly surprised that the producer had a copy of the 'Swansea Jack' story book, which he had read from cover to cover.

He seemed genuinely interested, and our talk developed in-depth, allowing me to expand on the local history of Jack and how his admiration was such that a memorial in his honor stands overlooking Swansea Bay. There was even a public house name after him; now sadly shut, or we may have been able to nab a few free pints.

The story had to be told, and Keith the member of the Maritime Volunteers, who accompanied us at sea for extra safety, was willing to tell it all in front of the camera. I think, actually, he only did it as he secretly yearned to be a stunt man driving a speed boat for James Bond, and here was his chance to air his good looks and seafaring expertise!

The BBC presenter, Michaela Strachan, was assigned to film with us, which was an excellent choice of a person. I had met her a few times before and found her to be a lovely relaxed person, who is so good with animals. Michaela used to live near to my home in North Somerset, not far from the beautiful town of Clevedon. She had attended a few fundraising events that our charity Newfound Friends, had put together to raise funds for the Little Bridge Children's

Hospice in Barnstable. I was hoping she would remember me.

With all the pre-arrangements made with the producer, we agreed to meet up at Swansea Marina on Sunday at 9.30 am, with the intention of locking out into the Bristol Channel at 10 am.

For now, it was time to go and eat, as Whizz was obviously reminding me with that knowing look. "Stop all that gassing, Dave, and let's make waves to Auntie Mary's and steak!"

Whizz's nose twitched. I am sure he could smell the aroma of minced steak and gravy wafting over the hill from Auntie's kitchen. Not a stampede of wild horses could stop Whizz from charging through the front door when there was food on offer. It was a good job the door was ajar, or it would be splinters at dawn; not that it would have worried Auntie, she thought the world of Whizz.

The gourmet meal was carefully arranged in a shiny stainless-steel bowl mounted on a raised stand. This eating position makes for better digestion for large breeds of dogs. Auntie Mary even complimented the feast with a rather palatable Welsh spring water purchased from the local market. I am surprised there weren't little doggie napkins and a matching tablecloth.

Was Whizz impressed? I do not think he even noticed and wolfed down the lot in seconds, much to our amusement. Suitably nourished, he retired to his favorite place – under the kitchen table on the cold flagstone floor. Comfy beds were pointless; he much preferred the coolness of the stones.

My canine companion was not the only one who was in need of sustenance. It had been a long day for me too, and I had a healthy appetite. I wondered if I was to be treated to steak. No chance of that; ushered I was, off to the fish and chip shop... and a very tasty supper it turned out to be.

As Whizz stretched out under the kitchen table beneath our feet, I told Auntie Mary of the plans for the next days' filming. Mary herself was an accomplished swimmer, representing Wales in the British and Empire Games in Cardiff in 1958 (now called the Commonwealth Games). She had a great affinity with both pools and the sea; it was good to have time to sit and have a good old natter.

We chatted about the great progress Whizz was making as a water rescue dog and the potential he had of becoming my best-ever swimming Newfoundland. My sleepy companion's ears pricked up at the mention of his name before he sussed out that nothing much was going on and resumed his slumber beneath the table.

We also talked about Swansea Jack and the legend of his rescue of the stricken puppies thrown into the murky water way back in the 1930s. It was a practice all too common; no vets, spaying, or castration in those days. Dogs ran free and had to be tough.

Auntie Mary said that she had never met Jack, but her father (my grandfather) Arthur Palmer, a timber merchant at the docks, had many a heroic story to tell of the famous black, curly-coated retriever. We always called Grandad Arthur 'Jim' – and that became his nickname, but my memories of him were not all that pleasant. He followed my mother when she moved over from Wales, and I am sure she had a lot to put up with. I still remember going to his house, the wooden toilet, condensed milk, and a large wooden mangle! It's strange what stays in your mind. What happened to my grandmother, I do not really know; I am sure there is a mystery there.

The tales surrounding Jack's heritage were murky. There was some talk of Newfoundland in his breeding, but it was more likely that Jack was a mixture of all sorts. He was owned by a haulage contractor named Mr. Thomas but, as with most dogs, spent most of his day foraging for tasty titbits lodged in nooks and crannies around the docks. Sadly, this would be his demise when he ingested rat poison and met his end.

He became the local hero, and tales of his rescues travelled far and wide. Many a story was told of his bravery, as he frequently swam into the docks, giving tows to the boys who leapt, time and time again, with their 'Tombstone' jumps, recklessly into the water. Whether this was classed as an actual rescue, who knows?

It is not for me to pour cold water on Jack's stories, and our charity Newfound Friends, made Jack our Dog of the Century in 2000. We also commissioned a painting of him in order that his stories would live on; he was a true legend of Swansea.

The parallels between Jack and Whizz run side by side; both have been awarded medals from the Dogs Trust and the PDSA. Jack raised monies for charity with a collection box around his neck. Whizz raised money with his sponsored rescues. Whilst Whizz does not have a memorial to him as yet; there has been an approach from Bill Lane, founder of the Just Giving Appeal and the Arts Council, for a statue of Whizz to be placed on the Quay of Poole Harbor. What a tremendous tribute that would be.

After a few glasses of red wine for me and a glass or two of Brains beer for Auntie Mary, there was much nostalgia in the air as we spoke of my family and my mother, Edith. Being eighteen years older than Mary, Mum was responsible for much of my aunt's upbringing and taught her to swim at the council baths in Swansea. Sadly, my mother passed away when I was in my late twenties, but as a great animal lover, I am sure she would have loved Whizz.

The merry banter went on and on, and it was Whizz's loud snoring that made us realize, it was way past our bed time.

As I opened the curtains of the bedroom early on a Sunday morning, the weather did not look good; an overcast sky and a blustery wind. It was my first job of the day to take Whizz for his early morning walk in the inclement weather, around the village of Bishopston and out into the recreation field to allow Whizz to run off some steam. The plan was to head off home to North Somerset after the filming, so it was swiftly back to Auntie's house in time for a quick coffee and a slice of toast.

Not so quick was donning the cold, damp wetsuit hung allegedly 'drying' from the previous day. There is nothing worse than putting on a cold and 'wet' wetsuit. I can only compare it to coming out of a hot shower and having to dry yourself with a dripping towel. Pulling it over your body is downright painful, forcing folds you never knew existed upwards and beyond to wrap like tribal ringlets around your neck. It is such a shame it did not work on the mush; a free facelift wouldn't half be good.

Eventually, dressed and ready, I loaded up my van with all my essentials and, of course, the one and only Whizz; said our fond goodbyes and set off on the short trip to Swansea's Marina, seeking more fame and fortune.

By the time I had parked in the Dylan Thomas Museum car park, close to the marina, I could see most of my friends and the team were up and ready. The boat was prepared for launch on the slipway; it was all green for go...We awaited the producer and film crew with excitement and a few niggly nerves.

I was particularly glad to see Natalia Budd, who, if you remember from the previous renditions of shenanigans surrounding the award ceremony a few years ago, had two brothers attending the children's hospice in Barnstable around that time. She became an integral part of the charity then and has helped massively with fundraising ever since. Any professional filming is exciting, and it was a small gesture I could make, after all she has done, to give her the opportunity of appearing on National TV. It would be something for her mother and father to treasure.

We did not have to wait long, and soon the BBC crew appeared with more equipment than a precautious astronaut would take to the moon. Introductions to all our personnel and the dogs were politely carried out. Polite is probably a good word, as all our dogs are well trained and friendly with each other... Until you come to the Battle of The Bulge... Yes Boswell had arrived, and how 'pleased' would Whizz be to see him!

Boswell, although owned by Tim, another member of the team, was on a par with Whizz – top dog. Tim suffered from panic attacks, and thus, it was I who trained and displayed with Boswell for a fair amount of time before Whizz arrived on the scene. I looked upon Boswell as my dog, and we shared that special bond between man and beast.

My fondness, as with all my dogs, was no less for Boswell when Whizz arrived and found a place at the top of the tree. I believe Boswell was not happy to share the pedestal, and likewise, Whizz was a tinge bit Jealous, perceiving the close relationship I had with his 'rival'.

Consequently, much growling and barking ensued as Tim quickly ushered Boswell passed the rear of the van, where Whizz was totally miffed at being still caged in. We were well used to their antics, but unfortunately, whatever you do to alleviate, some dogs do not get on with others...

like us, I suppose. It was best to keep them apart as much as possible, especially when they were working, and just put up with the verbals and intimidating glares of, 'stay away from me, or else!'

A taxi arrived in the carpark and outstepped our presenter for the day, Michaela Strachan. Any worries about recognition dispersed as she rushed over and gave me a welcoming hug and a kiss on the cheek. Lowering her face to the mesh, eyeing up the soppy look Whizz was giving as if to say, 'What about me?' Michaela smiled.

"And who's this handsome fellow?" she grinned.

"Whizz!" I replied proudly. "He's a new arrival and shows much promise. Do you remember Bear?" I asked.

Michaela had met Bear at the hospice on more than one occasion and was more than happy to natter away to Natalia, whom I called over to meet the TV star. There was no need for any awkwardness; Michaela has the sort of personality that puts everyone at ease.

Not everything went totally to plan, though. Keith Joseph, the unit commander of the Swansea Maritime volunteers, had taken advice from the coastguard; filming in the choppy sea was not going to be an option – the weather conditions were uncertain.

It was decided, with the relevant permissions, that it would be safer for all if we did all the 'Lights, Camera, Action' malarkey inside the marina in calm waters. It was a shame, as Newfoundlands work much better in the open sea, but health, welfare, and red tape insurance rules, quite rightly, dictate. We were disappointed, but the delight on the BBC crew's faces could not be hidden; I do not think they were relishing the waves.

Before any of us got wet, there was some dry land filming to take place; firstly, along the grassy verge that runs along Swansea's Promenade, taking in the Swansea Jack Memorial stone, and then with Michaela and Whizz on the beach. Whizz was a very powerful dog, and I had concerns that he would very easily pull the tiny Michaela Strachan over flat on her face. To my surprise, there was clearly an inner strength in the famous TV presenter, and she handled Whizz surprisingly well. (Either that or Whizz knew exactly how to play up to the camera – being the Divo he was).

The water displays went exceedingly well, with all giving outstanding performances worthy of doggy Oscars. Michaela and the team were pleased with the takes, and the recordings finished with obligatory slobber and a waft of Newfoundland sent in the air. The day was deemed to be a brilliant success.

I look back now on this sequence of the film with great affection and fond memories.

Whizz looked absolutely stunning, powerful with steely strength and determination, a far cry from the timid Bear lookalike, shuddering by the edge of the training lake all those years ago. It was amazing how love, affection, good food, and a true purpose in his life transformed him into a Prince of all dogs.

Funnily enough, this piece of film was purchased by the pop rock band 'Scouting for Girls' and was featured in their pop video of their song, 'Michaela Strachan'. There they both are as if Whizz had known Michaela for a year, strolling happily along the beach with not a care in the world.

Not many dogs can lay claim to being pop stars! It's a good job Boswell never found out; that really would have caused real problems, though I think, really, he is more of a Will.i.am sort of dog... 'Gimme a break; like; gimme a steak; like, gimme it now, or I'll jump in that lake!'

Whizz at Swansea beach

Chapter Ten: Whizz's First Rescue

It was whilst we attended one of our annual celebrations at the Sea Shanty Festival in Swansea that Whizz spontaneously carried out his first real-life rescue. Unlike the 'supervised' (well, almost) parachutists tangling disaster expertly dealt with in Cardiff Bay a couple of years later, when Whizz was a true expert in his field, this came completely out of the blue.

As with any event, even though we had repeatedly displayed at Swansea, each show had to be preceded by myself to ensure the health and safety of all concerned and, most importantly, the humans and dogs in the water.

At Swansea, Caroline Jenkins, events manager of the city council, was our first port of call (if you pardon the pun), and right from the very first festival, she took heed of all our concerns and, after the most pleasant of meetings, carried out our wishes with enthusiasm. This included checking whether the slipways were suitable for launch and also arranging bacterial tests for the occasionally murky-looking soup in the Marina. Thankfully we never encountered any problems, the tests were always clear, and Carline has become a trusted friend for over twenty-five years now.

This particular incident happened just before we were due to display at the Shanty festival. All was ready for the off as the team, and our friends watched as Gordon expertly launched the boat into the marina. Keith, head of the Volunteers Marine Service, Swansea was there also, always supportive of our cause, and as the team was well prepared, suitably donned in our wet suits, dogs harnessed and ready; there was still time for a bit of a chit chat and a wander or two amongst the crowds before our three o'clock slot.

Not far from the actual Marina, where the River Taw travels along its majestic journey to the open sea, is a somber-looking bridge spanning the main A4067 road connecting Swansea to the mumbles. It is known by the emergency services as the 'Jumper off the road bridge', a sad reminder of the numerous suicide attempts having been made from the fateful structure.

We were well in the midst of answering the usual questions from the public, like, "Well, do you walk or ride it?" and "Have you a second home for all the food you need to keep?" when there was an almighty commotion flaring up nearby.

People began waving, shouting, and pointing at the bridge.

"Man overboard!"

"Help, someone help!"

Keith, immediately recognizing the situation, ran over yelling, "It's a jumper!" – it was no joke or set up, and he wasn't talking about a cable-knitted cardigan.

We instantly knew that driving the boat to the bridge was not an option. The marina entrance was strewn with barriers to stop any unwanted flotsam attempting invasion from the sea and possibly damaging man and vessel; negotiation would be far too slow, and even at our fastest speed, we would not be able to scoot out of the marina and into the river by the bridge in time.

Gordon, Clive, and I wasted not a second, and without hesitation, all three of us legged it along the grass and down the grassy bank. We could see what appeared to be a young man, unconscious, floating face down in the water. There was no time to lose – in an instant, Clive and I plunged into the chilly course.

I did not realize, in our haste, that I had not secured the van, and Whizz, immediately sensing danger, flew open the doors and pelted after us at full throttle, oblivious to all in his path – my Whizz was a dog on a mission. On and on, he strove, overtaking us in the shallows, diving into the drink, swimming strongly and intuitively towards the victim.

The young man was not able to grab the harness, but Whizz swam in circles around him until we were able to reach the drowning casualty, turn his body upwards, and gesture to Whizz to do his job. The fearless canine, with his strength to tow twelve men, bravely made his way, all three of us clinging to the shore.

The sound of wailing sirens greeted our ears, and the repetitive flicker of blue lights flashed across our eyes as we carefully carried the young man to the river's edge. He was, thankfully, regaining consciousness but extremely groggy when the paramedics took over and, after their immediate assessments, transported him to the waiting ambulance and forward to the hospital.

Everyone clapped and cheered; Whizz had saved the day! Was he aware of it? I have no idea; he just lolloped around, as usual, shaking the gallons of water from the mop of his coat and soaking all and sundry – a favorite with the children who seemed to take great delight in getting an early shower.

As for the young man, we were told he had a concussion, and it was a response to a 'dare' that landed him and his onlooking mates in such hot (well cold) water.

The display went ahead, slightly delayed, but the crowd whooped with delight as the dogs showed off their talents, and it all resulted in a standing ovation.

After the inevitable police statements and a winding down of the day, it was a hose-down for the dogs and a belated warm shower for myself. To say it was an amazing afternoon would probably be inappropriate, given the circumstances of potential death, but I was so proud of Whizz that my heart could have burst. I think the team was certainly elated and in for a few jokes as the ladies invaded my naked self as I stood under the hot spray. Thank God they did not have waterproof cameras...

From then on, accepting Keith invitation, Whizz became an integral part of the Marine Volunteers, working alongside them as a lifeguard, parading the beaches and seas near Swansea and the Gower Peninsular whenever required, especially in peak holiday periods. There are no restrictions on dogs here, and unlike other parts of Southern England, it is relaxed and free for all our friends to enjoy these wonderful beaches though-out the year.

There were a few modifications to the craft to facilitate a canine sailor, chiefly, a raised platform to enable Whizz a safe take-off, covered by a tight-fitting, non-slip rubber to avoid accidents. I had found this out to my detriment some time ago... 'Ouch! That was a bit painful on the old butt' is the polite version.

So, why a dog, you may ask, is not a boat manned by a bunch of experienced seamen enough? Sometimes it would be, but an inflatable raft is prone to the elements of sudden winds and tidal movements. A Newfoundland is ultimately stronger and naturally able to negotiate the swells, cutting through the choppy waves like a knife through butter.

This does not mean we leave it all to the dogs; we would never put them in danger and never leave them to rescue alone. They still need precise training, and their job is to swim to the casualty calmly, not to cause panic, and leave the talking to the lifeguards who would not be far behind. If they were able, the victim would be encouraged to lie on their back, grab the harness, and the dogs would do the rest.

There is a unique way of rescuing a drowning person with a dog, the French told me years ago. Holding onto a person, crossing the casualty's left arm over their body and keeping in that position with the lifeguard's right hand. No one wants to harm anybody in a rescue situation unless all this is completely effective, and also least one arm is free for the lifeguard to help swim back, holding the dog's rescue harness.

A rescue dog would always tow with a rope in its mouth; no attachments, saving the harness, were ever strapped to the animals, and this would be extremely dangerous. I was very pleased that the Maritime Volunteers took on board (there you go, another pun!) my advice and Whizz became a well-known valued full member of the team.

The only other issue which arose in training with the volunteers were the dry suits. Perfectly adequate for the rescuers, keeping all snuggly and warm, but useless swimming in the sea, as Steph, on our first 'dry' (or wet) run. She found herself bobbing about in the water, zipped tightly in her bright yellow suit impossible, floating around like an overly inflated, chicken-flavored Walkers crisp packet... That was soon rectified – wetsuits for all.

Everyone was happy with the training exercises, and Whizz became the only water rescue dog working with a maritime rescue service, attracting a vast amount of media attention. He was fast becoming a celebrity in his own right, his handsome looks and incredible demeanour in demand.

He even played his part in teaching water safety to children, and we paid a visit to local schools, where his popularity was obvious to pupils and teachers alike.

What a dog Whizz was turning out to be! I could have exploded with pride. Like Swansea Jack, a loveable rogue that, through affection and friendship, made him the hero he was.

Newfoundland Friends awarded Jack the 'Dog of The Century,' and commissioned a portrait of Jack, painted by Anne Mainman, which hangs in Swansea Town Hall. I also met Mary Stickler, author of the book 'Swansea Jack' and friend of Jack's owner Mr. Thomas. How great would it be to do the same for Whizz? Well, we are halfway there!

Whizz to the rescue at Swansea

Chapter Eleven: Topper Comes a Cropper

January is the month I dread. Work is always quiet in my joinery shop, and if I don't get a run of contracts booked in before Christmas, I generally have to wait until March for an up-turn. The short, cold, dark days, coupled with muddy dog walks and tax returns, only add to the murkiness of my mood.

Whizz loved these cold days, though; all Newfoundland dogs seem to enjoy the bleak midwinter, and the bleaker, the better. A chill wind is a music to their ears, which flap with joy as they go bounding across the frost-encrusted fields and splattering through the muddy slush.

Even on the chilliest nights, Whizz, Bear, and Izzie often chose to escape through our very large dog flap (so large it was pretty much a door) and sleep outside in the courtyard. When we were bombarded with a big overnight snowfall – which doesn't often happen in the south of England – it was like Christmas had come again for the dogs. They loved it! Opening the courtyard door, I would scour the blanket of white and fail to spot the boys until suddenly there would be a minor earthquake, and they'd emerge from beneath a pile of the white stuff, shaking it all over me until I was a proper yeti.

I am sure our cottage, with its very thick walls, low ceilings, and large wood-burning stove, would be a warm and cosy place to live if only we could shut the doors to keep the heat within.

Unfortunately, Newfoundland dogs like total access to the outside world, and doors in their world need to be open. The island in eastern Canada where the breed evolved is a wild place where only the best equipped can brave the harsh extremes of weather. With their double-thick oily coats and large paws (perfect snowshoes!) Newfoundlands can easily survive anything an English winter can throw at them. Even on a walk in the woods, they're ready to tackle Everest.

That particular winter's day, Sunday, 28th January 2007, I rose as usual at 6.30 am, in pitch blackness. Despite the silence, I knew Whizz and Bear would be waiting downstairs in the kitchen, ears pricked for the thud of my feet on the stairs. Their early morning walk was my first job of the day, before any thoughts of coffee or breakfast, and they knew it.

"Come on then, boys," I murmured, half-heartedly pulling on my wellies and coat and slipping their leads on. Izzie looked up briefly but then rested his head back on the kitchen floor, not well enough to join us, poor old boy.

Outside, there was no snow, but the frost was slippery underfoot, and I trudged cautiously along the dark lane using a mixture of moonlight and habit to find my way until we reached the church path where I could let the dogs run free. Whizz raced on ahead just as Izzie used to do. Bear, a little less excitable, stuck closer to me, his breath hanging in clouds and his mighty paws crunching the frosty grass. No doubt, when the sun came up, fellow walkers would see the route we had taken.

As was the morning ritual, Whizz and Bear waited for me at the church gate, and we walked through the graveyard to the porch, where I said my prayers. The church was decommissioned in the 1990s and is now managed by a conservation trust, so the door is often locked, but the sheltered area does me fine for the reflections I need to make.

Do I believe? I think so. My family was Methodist, so, as a young boy, I had no choice but to attend church and Sunday school, and I think my formative years left a lasting image engraved on my mind. I do wonder what went through Whizz and Bear's brains as I mouthed my morning prayers, but perhaps they, too, were well-behaved Methodist boys just like I had to be! I like to think so.

Usually, we had the porch to ourselves, although I do remember one wintry morning when we disturbed a homeless man who had curled up on the cold stone bench for the night. Because it was dark, and nothing could be seen until we were very close, all of us jumped a mile. I bet he was pretty alarmed to come nose to nose with the hounds of the Baskervilles until he realized they were a pair of giant softies.

It was still too black to see the Gordano Valley that morning, but as we continued our walk up a sharp incline, we could see the lights of the cars and lorries roaring along the M5 motorway.

Soon, it was back home across the fields and down the lane to my cottage, completing a pleasant circuit of around fifty minutes. The boys went to their water bowls for a well-earned drink, then 'literally' went to chill out just outside the wide-open front door, giving them a great vantage point of the comings and goings in the village.

"Time for some breakfast," I announced, flicking on the kettle and firing up the hob.

I do try to eat healthily six days a week, but on Sundays, I allow myself a full English fry-up as a special treat. The crackle of bacon and the waft of sausages soon brought Whizz and Bear back inside, and even Izzie, who was on his last legs by then, heaved himself up and plodded over. My furry friends positioned themselves at the kitchen table and watched my fork intently as it tucked into the feast and brought each morsel to my lips...

The crowd observing a centre-court match at Wimbledon could not have been more precise. "New sausages, please, Dave!"

Avoiding eye contact did not work; I had no choice. "Oh, go on then," I groaned, passing Bear a rasher of bacon. "Just one." He gobbled it down in a flash.

Whizz nudged my knee as if to say, 'Oi! What about me?'

Grudgingly I offered him a rasher too. "Just one, mind, Whizz."

Then, of course, it was 'just one sausage' for each of them, plus a few morsels for Izzie, seeing as he had made an effort to get to his feet. Somehow, I was left with only eggs and toast. 'Humph'...

Turns out I ate the whole week healthily after all, with my dogs keeping such a close eye on my diet!

There was nothing much to do with the rest of that day except go for another dog walk. It was either that or staying in and catching up on accounts or doing my tax return.

Whizz, of course, would have happily gone swimming in a freezing lake, but there was little call for lifeguards at this time of year, so come lunch time I took the dogs out on a flattish circuit around the village. Just a short walk of twenty minutes, and then we would be back home for the rest of the day – or so I thought.

A couple of hours after we returned home, however, Whizz grew restless.

"Dave?" Jean called from the kitchen just as I was settling into my armchair. "What's with Whizz?"

I joined her at the doorway to the courtyard where Whizz was pacing up and down fretfully as if he had a best man's speech to write or something. He also kept pawing at our five-bar gate.

"Maybe he needs to go and relieve himself," suggested Jean.

It was 4 pm by now, and the light was fading fast; the last thing I fancied doing was going out in the cold and dark for a walk. What I really wanted to do was put my feet up by the wood-burner and watch a bit of telly, preferably until winter was over.

Whizz refused to settle, and eventually, I caved in and fetched his lead with all the enthusiasm of a lazy sloth, forced to compete in the three-metre race at the carnival of animals, annual sports-day.

Leaving Jean with Bear and Izzie, who were happily snoozing on the kitchen floor, I led Whizz up the lane behind our house, thinking it would be a quick trip to the woods.

The path follows a sharp incline through a tunnel under the motorway and onto a bridleway, which climbs up through the woods to a lane of posh modern mansions known locally as Millionaires' Row. I kept Whizz on his lead until I reached the bridleway, then let him free.

By now, it was getting harder to see, but thankfully it was not raining, and I dug my hands into my deep pockets (filled with dog biscuits) to fend off the cold wind. I thought Whizz would have a quick jig a round and a wee on a tree, then we could go home, but he seemed distracted.

A hundred yards or so along the uncomfortably steep and stony bridleway, we came to a broken gate where a barely legible sign reads 'private keep out'. As I have done for years, I completely ignored the sign and veered off here onto a flatter, more comfortable path that weaves through the trees.

In this quiet spot, off the beaten track, there is an abundance of wildlife, and many a time, I have startled a roe deer or spotted a kestrel looking down at me from a lofty perch. Whizz was busy sniffing the undergrowth as if he expected such an encounter, and it was on the tip of my tongue to inform him that the birds had flown to warmer climes and that the squirrels, badgers, and rabbits were hibernating when suddenly he took off like a bullet.

"Whizz? Whizz!" I shouted, looking in vain in the hope of seeing even the tip of his massive waggly tail.

Normally, because of his training, he was very responsive to my commands, but this time it was a classic case of Newfie selective hearing. Still, it was out of character for Whizz, and I knew something was up. I ran into the dark, dense wood, stumbling over tree roots and fighting through brambles, calling Whizz's name and straining eyes and ears for my dog.

Crashing into a clearing. I was just in time to see the flash of my dog's hind legs as he leapt into a pool of water with a great splash.

"What the...?" I raced to the water's edge and, to my amazement, saw Whizz swimming over to a smaller dog that was floundering in the water, only just head-high above the surface. Whizz grabbed the animal by the top of its neck and dragged it with ease to the edge, where he abruptly stopped... this was not a normal bank.

It was then that I realized their predicament. They were not in a natural pool with a gentle slope that they could simply climb up, but, in fact, inside a large concrete tank about half the size of a tennis court. It was one of the storage reservoirs built into the wooded hillside long ago to provide water pressure for Clapton Court, a grand estate at the bottom of the valley. From the woodland floor surrounding the tank, it was a sheer drop of at least eighteen inches to the water's surface.

The reservoir was just shallow enough for Whizz to stand on his hind legs and get a purchase on the side with his paws but not enough to haul himself out. The terrified smaller dog had no chance at all. Despite the bedraggled state of the poor animal, I could see he was a handsome red setter with a sleek ginger head and floppy ears.

There was no way they could get out alone. If Whizz had not got there in time, the smaller dog would surely have drowned, and if I had not followed Whizz, both would have suffered a watery grave.

Luckily, it was easy for me to loosen the whimpering setter from Whizz's grasp and place him gently onto dry land. Whizz put his front paws on the edge of the tank and used his back paws to push upwards while I, with much huffing and grunting, dragged him out, falling backwards with the effort.

He was no mean lightweight, and it was a feat in itself to rescue the 'rescuer', and I briefly thought if I pulled my back out, that would mean all three of us were in need, but, of course, you don't really dwell on that when your best friend is in trouble.

Safely on dry land, Whizz nuzzled my face as if to say, 'you all right, Dave?', then shook the water from his coat, giving me an icy soaking.

"Brrr! Cheers, Whizzy," I mumbled.

Whizz was fine, but the setter was trembling uncontrollably, and blood was pouring from a nasty cut on its back right leg. There was no other option but to strip off and make an impromptu bandage from my t-shirt, which I wrapped clumsily around his leg and secured as tightly as I could.

With a freezing night falling, time was of the essence. I put my coat back on, scooped up the setter, placed it gently around my shoulders like a wet scarf, and set off back towards the path and the village. Whizz seemed to understand the seriousness of the situation and stuck closely to my side.

It was a huge relief when we made it down the cobbly path, through the gloom, and onward to the start of the paved lane, which leads back down to the village. The weight of the setter on my shoulders was increasingly difficult to bear, and its wet coat oozed cold water that trickled all the way down my body until my underwear and socks were uncomfortably sodden.

Just before the motorway tunnel, I paused to catch my breath and reposition the poor dog on my shoulders as there was no way it could walk on its injured leg.

Out of the darkness shrieked a panicked voice – "Topper!"

I looked up and literally saw the light at the end of the tunnel – the beam of torches sweeping from side to side and the outline of two figures heading towards me.

"Topper, Topper!" a man and a woman were shouting with dread.

When they saw me, they cried out and came running, the woman reaching us first. I gently placed the setter on the grass verge, and the woman dropped to her knees and threw her arms around the shivering animal.

"Topper!" She pressed her face against his neck, murmuring thanks into his wet fur.

"We've been looking for him for two-and-a-half hours," cried the relieved owner.

It was only then I recognised Charlotte, a lady local to the village.

Topper needed urgent medical attention, and while she kept her pet warm in her embrace, her boyfriend ran back to get his car to rush her dog to the emergency vet.

It was gone five by the time Whizz, and I arrived back at the cottage. The powerful security lights lit up his shaggy coat, which was still dripping with water. I knew he would want to spend the night in the courtyard, and I did not want his coat to freeze solid, so there was only one thing for it.

"Blaster time, Whizz," I announced, heading to the garage to fetch the weapon.

Whizz just looked at me as if to say, 'here we go then, time for the astronaut wind tunnel simulation.'

The blaster is a very strong hair dryer suitable for large dogs, and in no time at all, Whizz was all dry and fluffed up like a sheep. He could have done with a bath, really, but unless I wanted to camp out for the night, that was not a practical idea, so a blow-dry it was to be.

Once he was sorted, I went for a nice warm shower and a change of clothes while Jean made a nice, welcoming cup of tea.

The next day, not long after I arrived at my joinery shop after our early-morning dog walk, I received a call from Charlotte, informing me that Topper was doing well and would be right as rain within a few days.

"Will you be in this evening?" added Charlotte. "We'd like to thank you and Whizz in person."

That night, Charlotte brought a host of dog treats round for Whizz (and Bear, too) and told us the whole story. Topper had been off his lead when a deer shot across their path, and the setter had taken up the pursuit, disappearing into the woods, despite their frantic cries for him to come back.

Just how Whizz had known the little dog was in danger, I could not really comprehend. Was it at that very moment when he took off into the woods, or had he sensed something earlier and from further away? It was odd he was so unsettled, even before I condescended to take him out. Was it intuition or coincidence? I guess we will never know, but it was a moment in time I feel sure I'll never experience again.

Certainly, Topper had made no cry for help as far as I heard. But dogs have senses we don't always understand, and Whizz must have picked up on something. The chances of someone just stumbling upon a redundant reservoir in a private piece of woodland in the last ten minutes of daylight on a cold January evening were one in a million, I would say, but then Whizz was a one-in-a-million kind of dog.

News of the rescue eventually reached the editors of the regional paper, the Western Daily Press. They wanted pictures of Whizz and Topper together and sent out a photographer to capture the pair.

In the frame that made page three of the next day's edition, Charlotte stands in front of our five-bar gate, holding Topper aloft while Whizz towers over them on the other side with his front paws hooked over the gate top, giving the setter a look of approval.

We could not have imagined the impact of that article, and things went completely crazy after that. Firstly, local radio and TV got hold of the story; then, the Bristol-based nationwide agency SWNS took their own pictures. The very next day, photos of Whizz and Topper were splashed across the national newspapers.

As with most scoops, the attention soon faded, and life returned to normal until, almost a year later, I received a phone call from the London-based Dogs Trust. Previously known as the Canine Defence League, the trust had a long and well-established history of dog welfare and was in the process of organising the very first Dogs Trust Honors.

"It's going to be a sort of doggy Pride of Britain Awards," the lady on the phone explained to me. "We'll be honoring dogs who have greatly helped their owner, or local community, or society in some way. We've heard all about Whizz's rescue of Topper, and we wondered if you'd be happy to attend?"

I looked out the window and spotted Whizz and Bear cooling off in the January sunshine. "We would be delighted," I replied.

The Dogs Trust pulled out all the stops for us to make it on 6th February 2008, a truly memorable day. We were offered free train travel to London, an overnight hotel, and even a chauffeured limousine to the awards ceremony at the prestigious Guildhall.

The free transport was a fantastic gesture but not one I could accept. A large lolloping shaggy dog slobbering on a train and in a very expensive limousine is not the best mix. The hotel offer, though, was gratefully received.

The awards bash was to be a black-tie evening; I did not really want to jaunt up to London in the van, all dressed up to the nines. That would be akin to being strapped to the driving seat in a strait jacket – and turning your head in that collar? A ventriloquist's dummy without his manipulator would have more success.

I was allowed to choose the hotel of my choice and, as I needed a car park without a height restriction (in respect of the van, I hasten to add, not myself – I am not that tall!) I, therefore, opted for a Travelodge in the Docklands, a few miles east of the City of London banking district, where the impending venue, the Guildhall, is situated.

Arriving mid-afternoon, I had plenty of time to let Whizz stretch his legs and enjoy some fresh air on his first-ever visit to the capital. Usually, when I'm out on dog walks, people make a beeline for us, eager to say hello and pat the enormous dog. In London, though, it was very noticeable that people kept their distance. What a sad and impersonal world they live in.

Back at the pet-friendly hotel, Whizz waited patiently while I got dressed up in my black tie (though mine was actually green), then we went downstairs to the lobby where my good friends Gordon and Karina, having travelled down from Cheltenham, were waiting.

They had happily snapped up my guest tickets and were more than enthusiastic about taking seats in the chauffeur-driven limousine. I even think I snipped a glimpse of Karina waving a queenlike arm as she glared excitedly at the carriage window.

Whizz and I followed in the van... something was not quite right there, the star of the show, dragging along behind the 'posh' guys.

"Okay, Whizz, I know it's not as great as the limo," I admitted to my canine friend, "but the aircon settings are just right for you. Sit back, chill out and stay cool."

The floodlit Guildhall looked spectacular on that February night. I had last visited the building several years earlier, at the end of my joinery apprenticeship, to pick up a City and Guilds gold medal as the southwest's top apprentice. The site of this magnificent structure rekindled fond memories and happy days. Tonight though, it was Whizz in the spotlight. I thought he might be a little fazed by the glittering crowd and clicking cameras that greeted us as we were ushered inside, but he took it all in his stride.

A slender man in a sparkly black suit and open shirt strode over and greeted Whizz like an old friend, and as soon as I heard that familiar Irish voice, I realized it was none other than Graham Norton, the host of the evening. A lot of so-called superstars can be standoffish with a big dribbling dog that sheds hair by the handful, but not Graham. He made a huge fuss over Whizz; I thought that was lovely.

There must have been a good three hundred and fifty people sitting down to dinner, and I saw many famous faces. Seated at our table alone were dancer Anton du Beke, comedian Sean Hughes, Office actor Martin Freeman, and the glamorous Linda Lusardi, to name a few of the people I first recognised.

I was just preparing myself with questions to ask any celebrities who might come and talk to me when the CEO of the Dogs Trust wandered over and introduced himself.

"Did you catch Blue Peter on TV tonight?" he asked.

I shook my head.

"Well, you were on it," laughed Keith.

I grinned. It seemed Alex Legger, our good friend on the show, had caught wind of the awards bash and re-run the clip of Whizz at the Trafalgar two-hundred celebrations before telling the viewers all about Topper's rescue.

Despite all the excitement and attention, Whizz was growing restless. I knew he would not be comfortable sitting at the foot of the table while I tucked him into a lavish dinner with wine, making small talk with Linda Lusardi & co.

(Well, who wouldn't?) I could well imagine what he was thinking.

'This is getting a bit boring now. Look at all those humans dressed up as penguins – and for what purpose? Are they going to have a good old swim in the sea later? I wish! How am I going to get out of this one, then? Right then, Dave, enough is enough. Stop chatting up the ladies, and let's get out of here. Thinking of all that ocean, there's only one solution – Whizz conveniently needs a Whizz!'

"Come on, boy, let's get some fresh air." I pushed back my chair.

Whizz followed me out of the function room, and we stepped out into the cold February night, pausing by one of the huge stone columns that hold up the doorway of the iconic landmark building. The temple pillars, impeccably decorated with ornate carvings, stood majestically tall; it must have taken days of artistic expertise to construct. Well, that was too much temptation for Whizz, who, eyeing up this over-embellished lamp-post, promptly cocked his leg and peed all over it.

I am not sure if it was the call of nature or a mark of his displeasure at being confined in a stuffy hall – I feel possibly the latter. The damp patch was quickly mopped up, and as far as I know, Whizz must have made a lasting impression, as there hasn't been a dog award ceremony held at Guildhall since.

While Gordon and Karina tucked into a sumptuous dinner, washed down with wine, I sat in the cool van with a can of coke and a Twix, patiently waiting for the glorious moment when Whizz would take to the stage and receive his award.

The story of Topper's rescue was projected onto a big screen behind us, and as we stepped up to receive the Dogs Trust Honor, the crowd erupted into a huge standing ovation. I am not one to get over-emotional at these things, but Gordon could not contain his joy. He leapt to his feet and punched the air.

"Woohoo!" he yelled. "Yeah!" And though I was too embarrassed to join in with him, I loved him for that.

It must have been well after midnight when the limousines arrived to take the guests back to their hotel after a night of photos, filming, and interviews that I will never forget. Gordon stayed with Whizz while I nipped into a cloakroom in the Guildhall and changed out of my tux for the drive back home. I knew Whizz would not settle in a hot hotel room, so I waved goodbye to Gordon and Karina and then hit the road.

On came the aircon; on came the radio. The bright lights of the capital were soon far behind us, and three hours later, we were back in the tranquil darkness of our North Somerset village. Bone tired and ready for bed, we still fizzed with pride and joy after that very special evening in London.

Whizz and Topper after the miraculous rescue

Chapter Twelve: Toni Curtis and the Cabbage Patch

I was always in awe of Whizz's ability to sniff out trouble before any human realized the onset of the crisis in the water, and it was during a very hot and action-packed bank holiday weekend of the Cardiff Bay 2009 festival his life-saving talents saved the day, yet again.

Some team members fancied extending the festival weekend into a full-blown holiday. Gordon and Karina decided to make a week of it and site their caravan near the beach in Swansea, and Debbie and her children joined them shortly afterwards. Tim and Boswell travelled daily and transported Vicki from her home in Fishponds, Bristol.

Vicki joined our association after watching the Newfies perform the previous year. She had a natural love and affinity with water and the dogs and was an incredibly lovely woman. Fitting in with our family immediately and proving to be an exceedingly valued member of the team.

Coincidently she lived in a converted shop on the corner of my childhood home street. Gone were the old dusty curtains and the drab brown of the frontage now. Still, it invoked nostalgic memories of my young days – the things you always remember – like the day you conquered a two-wheel bike or your very first kiss. I do not recall the bike much, but I do the kiss; it was with the delectable Nancy Jackson, who, so enthralled with my advances, emigrated to Australia shortly after.

With most of the team already there, that left me to tackle the holiday traffic with two large Newfies slobbering down my neck. I say 'two', as on this occasion, as well as Whizz, I now had in tow 'Ted'. Ted, indeed; the young juvenile; excitable, exuberant, and a real character. You could really describe Whizz as 'nautical and nice,' and Ted...well... 'nautical and downright naughty.' I was hoping Ted would learn from Whizz – which he did – water skills, but little else!

As is turned out this weekend, Whizz carried out a stunning, intuitive rescue and attempted another requested redemption of his 'little brother', of which he was less enthusiastic...

We arrived, after an extended two-and-a-half-hour holiday trip from hell, hungry and exhausted, at my favorite Auntie Mary's house on the outskirts of Swansea. She was always pleased to see us all and was not bothered by their antics... What are a few desecrated flowers amongst friends?

As was usual, Auntie laid on a magnificent spread of roasted Welsh lamb and vegetables while the boys, content after their normal, healthier meals, slept lazily on the cool conservatory floor. I will never understand how they could peg completely out, yet, the whiff of any food or the sound of a pin drop could open an eye in the hope of attention, but they had no chance with Auntie Mary's home cooking; it was devoured by the human form.

We were well prepared for the festival, held on the Saturday of that weekend, as we had taken part in this event many times. The day went off without a hitch, our dogs performing outstandingly, much to the delight of the crowd, who thundered approval with loud applause. I was well pleased with the whole affair, and we returned to Aunties house, tired but jubilant about our success.

Again, Auntie Mary came up trumps, fussing over her little 'angels' (one little angel and one little devil if you ask me!) while I gorged on huge amounts of mouth-watering sustenance. Soon the dogs were snoring away, and I was grateful for a comfy bed. The exhilaration surrounding these events was phenomenal, but this weekend, being a bank holiday, we had the added bonus of an extra day.

I awoke at 6 am to glorious sunshine and a certain 'Whizz', having slept by my side all night, stuffed his hairy chops right in my face, demanding the customary morning walk.

Being a frequent visitor, I knew the area well, and soon we were out into the fresh air, walking along the country way and onwards to a shady lane, safely fenced on either side, protecting the local council allotments. Here, it would be perfect for letting the dogs off the lead; no danger of any harm here...allegedly.

Ted, being 'Ted', managed to spot a small gap in the fence – only a rabbit robber armed with a magnifying glass would have seen the invitation. In an instant, he was gone, through the hole and into the prized gardens of Babylon; and heaven stood before him.

Lines and lines of uniformed furrows enticed his gaze. Lines and lines of strategically spaced, cervical planets of green vegetable delights. Yes, you guessed, more footballs than you could ever dream of, and it was 'Game on!'

I had no choice but to force my way through the gap, with Whizz following on – We could only stand and stare. Terrible Ted, of course, was in his element. Four massive paws and a head big enough to catapult a cannonball to Mars were far more effective than eleven pairs of boots striving to ram a disintegrating Savoy into the net coverings of the fruit bushes at the end of the small holding.

"Goal!!!" was not the words erupting from my lips at the time.

Whizz just sat there as if to say, 'Ah well, that's it then, that's Ted, up to his tricks again.'

I did not know whether to laugh or cry. Prized vegetables were everywhere, the perfect 2D shapes of the plots destroyed. The whole garden had been turned into a track fit for the Italian motor cross international championships...complete with strands of instant Ratatouille.

"Whizz!" I bellowed. "Go rescue your brother before we get arrested!"

"What?" Whizz looked at me in disbelief, "You want ME to carry out a vegetable mercenary mission? With that maniac and not a drop of water in sight – are you mad, Dave?"

"Just get him, Whizz!" That was a mistake.

Whizz, deciding that a rescue may be in order, after all, trampled swiftly across the apocalypse, making it ten times worse. In the end, I flew after both of them, eventually securing each by their leads and legging it down the path before anyone saw us.

"Fat lot of good you two are!" I gasped," What are we going to do if we get done for this lot? I know, we'll blame it on moles – BIG moles."

Safely away, I paused, leaned over, resting hands on my knees, squashing the leather between my fingers, fighting for breath. The doting duo sat patiently and watched me suffer as if nothing was amiss whatsoever. I looked at them; they looked at me, and I just burst into laughter.

By the time I had made it back to Auntie Mary's, my appetite for breakfast had disappeared. Despite the outwardly jovial response, I was conscious of the damage and not in the best of moods. Auntie, Magnificent Mary, thought the whole episode exceedingly amusing. Ted, with his handsome looks, was a real lady charmer, and he could get away with murder with one dewy glance.

"Never mind." She grinned, "At least you killed the weeds."

"Killed the weeds?" I wheezed, "and every other sodding plant in the ground. He's naughtier than Grandfather Jim!"

"No one's naughtier than your grandfather," giggled my aunt.

That was true enough. My grandfather, Jim, was a rather 'colourful' character. Banned from every pub on the planet, he was not a pleasant man, and I did not like him in the least. He also had a very angry, snappy little terrier, and the two complimented each other perfectly. I do not remember the name of the dog, but he should have been called 'Jaws'.

I think his character was inherited by my brother Richard. I distinctly remember one incident where both of us, together with Richard's friend David, were taken by my mother to visit my grandfather. Whilst I suffered the old man's presence, Richard and David were supposed to be playing in the garden.

It turns out they had destroyed the neighbor's prize marrow, lovingly nurtured for the up-and-coming local show. The overly large, angry man, brandishing a huge spade, chased them into my grandfather's house. I was expecting some chastisement of the boys, but all my grandfather did was set his dog on Goliath's ankles and laugh his head off!

I remember my mother gaping and shocked. This was not the behavior she endorsed; after all, his daughters portrayed none of his vile traits. Could I compare my grandfather to Ted? Thinking again, Ted was hard work, but I suppose not quite as bad!

My spirits lifted, and I downed my coffee and prepared for my departure from my Aunties house and a day at the beach before heading home. I was very much looking forward to a fun time with the team at one of our favorite haunts, Oxwich Bay.

Goodbyes in abundance, with the request to return in a couple of weeks – without Ted the Terrible -we set off on the five-mile journey to the sands. Before negotiating the narrow lanes to the coast, I drove gingerly, passed the allotments. Thankfully the gates were closed, goodness knows what state they were in, and I did not particularly want to see the atrocities.

Oxwich Bay is a beautiful, private beach nestling on the coast on the edge of Oxwich estate. There is a fee to pay on entry, and the rules are strict on the boat launch. An annual licence fee has to be paid to the landowners, and they also require proof of insurance and qualifications in maritime law and skills. Of course, we have all of this and more, and happy to provide it. You see so many unqualified and inexperienced people taking to the water in boats and jet skis – not a good idea and can result in great difficulties in the sea.

I found a shady spot to relieve the expected heat of the bank holiday sun, and the team arrived full of enthusiasm. They were even more delighted when I renditioned the tale of Ted's scoring sensation at the allotment stadium, sending them all into fits of giggles – seems like I was the only one to be embarrassed by my mutt's behavior; but to be honest, by then, I was also seeing the funny side once again.

Phoning Swansea Coast Guard to warn them that we would be launching our boat and doing various rescue exercises with the dogs off the beach and out into the sea was not only polite but advisable. It was a precaution to avoid any adverse reaction from the other people enjoying the beach, some of which would not understand the goings on.

Whilst Gordon steamed on ahead in the 4x4 boat and trailer in tow to launch the boat directly from the sands into the ocean, the rest of the team relaxed and relished food and drink from the small café situated at the far end of the beach.

Taking the dogs for a walk to stretch their legs, Whizz was his usual happy self, whilst Ted had no chance to cause any more trouble – a tight lead it was. That was the easy start to the training – putting on my wet suit was another matter. It never gets any better donning wet rubber; you think I would have learned by now that drying it out after use was essential. If I carry on being forgetful, my skin will be so stretched I could be mistaken for ET.

For the first couple of hours of training, we used Boswell whilst the other dogs stayed in the shade, with van doors wide open and constantly monitored by the rest of the team. Whizz would get his turn later, and I was not about to let the two fighting warriors meet; haddocks at dawn were not on the menu.

Boswell, Gordon, and our team member, Karina, manned the boat and circled the bay. I was to be the 'casualty' and wallowed in the waters outside the exclusion zone. The 'rescue' was carried out to perfection. Twenty meters away from my drowning self, Karina expertly released Boswell, who naturally flew through the air and landed in the sea with an almighty splosh. Swimming directly to me with no time to lose, I grabbed his harness and was towed to the safety of the craft.

Lots of praise and patting ensued, though Boswell was not really bothered. 'All in a day's work, mate', he merrily portrayed, as he soaked everyone, shaking off the residual briny pools.

All the dogs had their equal training time, and we tried to make it as fair as possible. By lunch time, the nitty gritty was completed, and time for food and some fun and frolics for us childish adults. The dogs were tired by then and quite happy to chill out around the vans, each of us taking turns to supervise.

Thankfully for us, the beach was not as crowded as anticipated. Apparently, there had been some accidents on the road, causing chaos, and many people turned back. Sad for them, not for us, more room to maneuverer! Out with the doughnut and on with the mayhem!

The massive tyre-like contraption is towed behind the boat whilst two of three of us pile upon it to keep it sort of stable. To be safe, though, a member of the team always holds onto the rope, just in case, it has to be released from its attachment. It is great fun, and adults and children alike take their turns, not always patiently waiting.

The shouts of 'ME NEXT! ME NEXT!' could probably be heard in Cardiff – and that was only the grownups.

After an exciting day, it was time to pack up and retrieve our boat onto its trailer. Gordon made a quick change out of his wetsuit as I stood by the boat with team-mate Vicky, with Whizz by my side, talking to a young couple interested in the dogs and Newfound Friends.

The boat was already winched onto the trailer and secured when Vicky suddenly shouted. "Whizz! What are you doing?"

Whizz did not hear; he was on another mission, pelting into the sea and swimming with all his might out towards the horizon.

Now, if that were Ted, I would have been distraught. Terrible Ted would have probably spotted some seaweed-sodden buoy bobbing on the waves, thinking it was another cabbage, but this was Whizz, and something was certainly wrong.

We do not normally let our dogs into the sea unaccompanied, and I was very worried as I knew the boat was unable to be relaunched quickly. However, Whizz had spotted someone in trouble. Straining our eyes, directed by a bystander, we could see a person struggling in the water. Thankfully, Whizz still had his harness on; we all bellowed as loud as we could, waving our arms wildly in the air.

"HOLD ON TO THE HARNESS. HOLD ON TO THE HARNESS!"

Whizz; my wonderful Whizz, single handily (well, four-pawed), circled the troubled swimmer, allowing her to grab the harness and tow her majestically through the turning tide, into the shallow waves, and unceremoniously to our welcoming arms. She was a young lady, visibly shaken and perturbed. It was essential to get her into the warmth to avoid serious shock.

With Karina and Vicky supporting her every move, we were able to guide her to the café, where she was wrapped in the foil blankets I always carried in our first aid kit. Concerned café staff rushed over with hot mugs of tea, chiefly for the young lady and then for all of us.

The crowds had gathered round and were parted by the appearance of a middle-aged gentleman, informing us, very loudly, that he was a doctor. Thank goodness there was one there when you needed him most, contrary to when you want to make an appointment at the surgery.

A quick assessment proved to be positive in its outcome, and apart from the obvious shock, the young lady was pronounced fit enough to avoid the hospital and just needed time and space to recover.

As for Whizz, the rescue was all part and parcel of his life; this is what came naturally and what he was trained to do. The intuition, however, never ceases to amaze me, however many times I say it. I have never known it so strong in any dog ever; Whizz was one in a million.

Eventually, things calmed down, the onlookers dispersed, and it was a much calmer person that informed us that she had decided to swim alone, to clear her head of some personal family problems; then been caught unawares in a riptide and swept out to sea.

Cuddling up to Whizz, thanking him over and over again for saving her life, you could see the gratefulness in her expression.

"My name is Toni Curtis," she beamed into Whizz's eyes.

Whizz cocked his head... 'What? Not THE Tony Curtis, Dave, have I saved a celebrity then?'

Toni gave his neck another squeeze as if to understand. 'No, not THE Tony Curtis, just plain old me, who is lucky to be alive.'

Ironically, Toni did become a celebrity. The media went berserk, her story being told on National TV and in all the papers. She was compelled to tell her story over and over again, to the extent that it all became a little too much for her. The dramatic accounts are great to hear, but enough is enough when you are reliving an experience that brings trauma to the surface every time you think about it.

At the end of her last ever TV interview, she uttered the words that make everything worthwhile.

"I will always be indebted to Whizz. He saved my life, and my three children still have a mother."

I have never been prouder of my Whizz at that time; he really saved FOUR lives that day.

Naughty Ted gives Carol Voderman a crafty lick much to Carol's amusement

Chapter Thirteen: Whizz and Ellie Bedford

Part 1

There are some people that instantly ooze natural affinity with their furry friends. Ellie Bedford was once of those humans who, even at the tender age of eleven, was destined for Newfoundland partnerships.

Ellies's parents, Adam and Trisha Bedford, contacted Newfound Friends, as they had welcomed their first all-black Newfie, Amy, into their lives and were seeking to teach her to swim. They were also very interested in becoming involved with the charity and introducing their daughters Ellie and her younger sister Chloe to the joys of doggy paddle exploration.

We arranged for the whole family, including Amy, to visit our training lake in Fairford, Gloucestershire, where the enthusiasm erupted in abundance and fun was had by all. Amy needed no encouragement – second nature for her!

Several visits later, after the purchase of one mini and one not-so-mini wetsuit (Ellie had a strong muscular build), the girls had quickly conquered the initial freezing-the-toes-off syndrome and taken to the water like a pair of excitable mallards.

Of course, there was love between all the Bedfords and their own Newfie, Amy; but the bond between Ellie and Whizz was immediately apparent. At three years old, my hero was already super experienced and capable of interacting with humans and animals of any age; (apart from squirrels, that is...squirrels were born to be chased). Ellie was no exception, and although Whizz was, quite honestly, being used to several partners, he was happy to swim with an ailing herring if it meant he could stay in the water; this time, though, it seemed he was determined to progress his career into teaching.

Safety, as always, was the most important, and I suggested the girls join a life-saving club to gain essential skills to enable them to be more independent in the water. Initially, both children were closely supervised until we were sure of their capabilities and comfortable with life jackets. Adam found a group close to their home in Shirvington, Oxfordshire, and the girls trained there for a number of years to gain their life-saving qualifications.

This did not stop them from partaking in the meantime, and although Chloe was enjoying her time with Newfound Friends, it was Ellie who shone the light. It was just a few months after she came to us, on a grand day in 2006, Ellie made her first public appearance with Whizz.

The venue was Portishead Marina, a relatively new conversion from the miserable, dreary dock. Previously serving the old coal-fired power station, it was still a little daunting, with its tall, stone, weather-worn walls and murky grey waters.

Swimming was not allowed in the marina, especially dogs; therefore, we were pleased to be asked to take part. My good friend Keith Berry, CEO of the marina, organized the whole event, chiefly a celebration for the berth holders and also a great opportunity to promote charity and show off our skills.

After surveying the dock, I decided the best place for her debut was to start the display from the long pontoon, facilitating the stack of boats tied securely before they locked out of the marina. Keith had arranged for the essential safety boat to be on hand to ensure no boats encroached on our movements and react quickly in any emergency. We would use this for our casualty 'recovery' vessel.

I could see Ellie was taken aback when I suggested, with Whizz by her side; she should start the display – I had every confidence in her ability. Some people would think that allowing such a young girl to swim with a very large and powerful dog was reckless. However, Whizz was exceptional, with proven success beyond expectations. I knew he was the one to guide her and keep her safe, as he had done many a time during practice.

With lots of encouragement and the assurance that Whizz would be by her side and we would jump together, Ellie overcame her reservations and, with our team member already 'drowning' in the water, prepared for take-off. A restricting life jacket was not an option during a rescue as it impaired a life saver's swimming action, so Ellie, contrary to my usual black attire, wore a wet-suit which gave her a fair amount of buoyancy in the water.

We must have looked like a pair of Michael Jackson groupies as the black and white trio ran along the pontoon and flew through the air. What a height this young eleven-year-old girl achieved with Whizz; it was outstanding! A perfect landing ensued, and I was able to swim at a safe distance, ready to intervene if necessary, but there was no need.

Ellie swam alongside Whizz towards the casualty, and I am sure I saw a little turn of his head as he made sure his partner was 'keeping up'. This did not detract from his objective in the least; it seemed multi-tasking was another skill that came to the surface – Whizz knew what he had to do to rescue the person in need and also give Ellie reassurance and confidence. Thus, with Ellie by his side, the pair of rescuers swam directly to the casualty, who grabbed the harness and was promptly towed by his canine saviour to the safety boat.

Our young friend was in her element and beamed with elation as she hugged Whizz, cuddling him as close as she could to her soggy colleague.

Whizz gave her a nuzzle. "That's okay, Ellie, you passed with flying colours – I think you are going to make a great lifeguard!"

As it turned out, he was exactly right, and Ellies's life-saving career took off – literally.

Our connections with the media had been well established as early as 2005, a few months after Whizz arrived to join our team. Paul Gillies, a very talented photographer for the Western Daily Press, came along to take photographs of all the Newfoundlands in action. His equipment, provided by the newspaper, was top of the range, and he knew exactly how to use it to its full potential.

One particular picture he took, of Whizz, flying through the air from the boat, has been used time and time over again. It was a cracking shot and was nominated as the BBC photo of the day that year. No amount of technology since has enabled anything to match the photograph.

Things expediated in the media rapidly after the publication and success of Paul's work. Whizz was enhancing his celebrity status almost on a daily basis...I am not sure if he recognised himself in the papers; I could have sworn I saw a flick of the forehead fringe at one time. It was a good job we did not have a mirror in the conservatory, or we would never have dragged him out of the house.

In late 2006 we were contacted by Martin Allard, who offered us a contract with a national newspaper for exclusive shots of our training and displays; this was signed and delivered in early January 2007. These things take time to arrange, and to obtain the most exciting coverage, good sunlight and excellent surroundings were a must. It was good luck we were arranging the year's events at the time, and we, therefore, decided to wait until July, returning to our beloved Oxwich Bay, by which time Ellie was flying high.

We always seemed to be blessed with glorious blue skies and calm winds at Oxwich, and the beautiful summer day in that July was no exception. The long, gently sloping, sandy beach is perfect for launching directly into the sea, and thus the inflatable rib easily slipped from its trailer into the lightly rippling waves. The bay is also a perfect environment for the dogs, safe and plenty of room for them to train and have a bit of fun.

When Martin arrived, I must confess, I was a little disappointed at the lack of equipment. Considering the potential extent of the publicity, I wondered if he would manage to obtain the wonderful quality of shots produced by Paul. A small digital camera seemed a far way off Paul's expanse of gadgets, especially as he had excellent connections with all the national newspapers – but Martin seemed confident and professional.

Landseer (Black and White), along with brown Newfoundlands, tend to produce the best action photos; black solid-colored dogs are more difficult to photo, although, with modern technology, this has become less of an issue in recent years. Martin had the opportunity to photograph all of the dogs we took along to partake in the day's events; however, it seemed the focus was definitely on our star Whizz.

Not all the dogs take to swimming in the sea; some do, some don't; each took their turn, but Whizz was in his element, and he just loved the open expanse of the sea with its salty water and wind in his furry coat. Flying from the boat at high speed to the rescue of anyone who chose to be a part of the action pictures, Whizz splashed into the sea to do his job time and time again. The team loved every minute, particularly young Ellie, who, at the ripe old age of twelve, had the confidence of a more mature life saver. The fact that photos and potential media exposure were on the menu, neither of them seemed to give a monkey; they were buzzing.

Whizz lapped it all up with delight, eager to jump with any of his team members; it was a feat in itself to restrain him as he repeatedly barked at his partners, anxious for the off –

'Come on, Ellie! Give it some wellie!'

Martin, constantly snapping his little camera, nineteen to the dozen, seemed pleased with his efforts, promising an email with the results later that week on the day snapping photos of the dogs and said that he would email some to us later in the next week.

The day on the beach was a huge success and thoroughly enjoyable, as we finished off with some jovial romps and games on the sandy shores.

I had no need to worry about the photographic coverage; it was incredible. He edited and wired them to each and every picture desk, offering them for sale. I well remember the day it all kicked off, August 8th, 2007, my auntie Mary's birthday.

Actually, it was pretty hectic the day before, with a host of journalists telephoning for a story behind the shots. I was not sure which and how many of the photographs they were going to use, but I gabbled on with as much information as I could muster from my overloaded brain – the story of Ellie and how Whizz had nurtured her into the confident partner she had become, was forefront. I could not have imagined, in my wildest dreams, what met my eyes when I looked at the papers the following day. Every national paper published the pictures and story of Whizz, many of them full-page features, both in paper and online format. It was sensational; the queen could not have been more popular that day.

As I made my way to work in Bristol, to my joinery workshop, my mobile phone rang constantly. I do not take calls when I am driving (I do not want to meet God just yet,) and so it was I had nine missed calls when I pulled up outside my business.

Enquiries flooded in from all kinds of establishments; publishers wishing to use the photos, Radio stations, TV companies, and also the general public. No chance of any carpentry that day; I could not have anticipated the extent of the response in a million years. I thought for one minute I was wasted making windows and should have whittled a hundred Whizz ornaments instead!

It was impossible to interact with them all, and despite the affiliation with the BBC, I decided that we would give ITV news the option to film us. We had a previous association with the Local HTV news way back in 1996, and it was the same presenter, Lisa Tatum, weather reporter then and now with Good Morning Breakfast News, that contacted us. Having swum with our dogs all those years ago, she had not forgotten her experience and was excited to be involved in further filming.

This turned out to be a godsend, as Lisa knew how the dogs worked, under what conditions, and all the paraphernalia that goes with it, certainly, saving a lot of time. It was agreed, as they wished to film as soon as possible, that the broadcast would take place at our training lake in Fairford. The only hurdle we had to conquer was obtaining permission form the United States Air Force!

Why? You may ask, all we were intending was to fly through the air close to the water, not encroach on any air space – Whizz jumped high, but not that high!

Longdoles lake was very close to the RAF base and leased to the United States Airforce. Normally, not a problem; you just had to be careful of low-flying aircraft in case it spooked the dogs – or us. Try having a leisurely swim and suddenly being frightened by a thunderous roar, and stunk out with fuel odour, shot out by a jet on a mission. The issue on this occasion was with communication. A live broadcast required a satellite connexion to the outside world, and the USA could be quite touchy about those kinds of things.

It took Lisa two whole days to achieve authorisation. Maybe they thought we could be spies; who knows? The nearest I ever got to a martini 'shaken, not stirred' was at the award ceremony in London when I was cocooned in a black noose and a straitjacket, hardly MI6, more like a man in a van – M4.

As it was a breakfast news program, I needed to set off with Whizz in the middle of the night on August the eleventh for the Friday morning program. Arriving at the lake around 5.45 am, ready for the first live slot at 6.20, I was pleased to see all was set up, including the 'spy' satellite truck.

We were scheduled to do three live shots at 7.45 am and the final at 8.50, so we needed other members of the team on hand; Ellie, of course, Gordon and his wife Karena, and Ellie's father, Adam. The casualty was to be the reporter, which we kitted out in a wetsuit, ready for action.

The cameraman zoomed in as close as he could as Whizz and Ellie carried out the 'rescue' with their usual precision. Their showmanship was faultless on all three repeats, and topping that success, were the interviews with Kate Garraway via our technological ear pieces. I was very proud of Ellie that day; being nervous as anyone would, she answered the questions with outward confidence.

Quite rightly, some of the questions regarding such a twelve-year-old girl and the dangers of working as a lifeguard reared their head once again, but I was ready to reiterate my feelings on that! I would never put anyone at risk and had total confidence in Whizz as a protector and a mentor to Ellie. She learned from Whizz's leadership and example, and it worked.

Learning by osmosis does not always work, though, as I found out to my detriment when I was six years old. It wasn't my fault that Dad had the brainy idea of starting a bonfire with a petrol-infused lighted rag – that worked fine. It didn't work fine when my friend David and I tried the same thing the very next day in the lane between our two houses. Suffice it to say, David's parents were stripped of their shiny black Ford Consul, and their garage was reduced to a smoking, charred hard standing. Trying to defuse the situation by assuring both sets of parents that we were both unscathed did not go down at all well – we were still in big trouble.

The moral of the story, then, is, to make sure when you are role modelling, you think about it properly and do not take risks. We all learn from our mistakes, that's life, but that was a big one! Not so with Whizz and Ellie; the partnership was amazing.

After the excitement of becoming a TV celebrity, things returned to normal. I went back to work, and Ellie continued to train with Whizz and the other Newfoundland dogs. Every Sunday, she continued to progress to her qualifications with the Royal Life Saving Society in Wantage. Her dedication and enthusiasm were relentless; unusual for a young person of her age when so many other projects tempt their interest.

The calm did not last for long. 2008 was a blast.

Part 2

Celebrity status

It was the year 2008, and our two celebrities were destined for stardom.

The news program was over and done with; it was back to the day job for me, and for Ellie, it was the school summer holidays. She continued to train with Whizz and the other Newfoundland dogs in the team, and every Sunday, she made considerable progress with the royal life-saving society with Wantage lifesavers. Young people often get waylaid by a new challenge or project, but Ellie never lost her enthusiasm to train with the dogs. Week by week, Ellie was making good strides with the team learning all the time and growing in confidence to prepare for her next appearance on the BBC 'One Show'.

Whizz was also coping with his new found celebrity status, taking everything in his own calm, laidback way. However, I was sure he was secretly harboring materialistic longings... for one day, he decided to move house.

Not content with his lovely, chocolate box cottage, set in the wonderful countryside of North Somerset, he had his eyes on a more majestic abode, nestled amongst the small group of celebrity dwellings, not far from our village.

Thus, it was that one morning, he took a massive leap over a five-bar gate and ran off towards the rich community to seek his fortune. Thankfully, Tom, our postman (who, incidentally, had swum periodically with the team) recognised the escapee, popped Whizz into his little red van, and returned him to us early in the morning... 'Postman Tom and his black and white chum' rang in my ears for days.

From the very start of 2008, it was clear this was going to be a momentous year for our charity Newfound Friends. We were bombarded with a host of invitations from many sources, one of which was most unexpected. The Jersey Tourism Board wondered if Whizz and the team would like to travel over to the island in the summer to do a display in the Marina.

As with all the new venues, we always do a reconnaissance visit to be sure that it is practical and safe for the dogs and the members of the team. The head of tourism completely understood and was willing to fly me over to take a look at the Marina and the practicalities and logistics of getting the dogs to Jersey. The board had a huge pulling power with the airlines, and my flight from Exeter airport was consequently arranged with Flybe UK.

On a cold early February morning, I caught the flight and, on arrival, met with Amy, the tourism officer. It was a golden opportunity for me to see the islands, and a quick tour was very welcome.

Over a pleasant lunch, we discussed practical arrangements. Amy had already pre-empted most of my concerns and had obtained an agreement that Flybe would charter one of its aircraft for both dogs and humans...what you can get when you are a celeb!

The risk assessment at St Helier marina was another matter. The marina manager seemed apprehensive about the whole thing, and although the marina was very large, it was crowded with boats moored to its numerous jetties. There was one clear space, which I felt would be safe enough, and

I hoped my persuasions would bear fruit. No immediate decision was made, and I left it all in Amy's capable hands to use her powers of coercion.

Unfortunately, it turned out not to be; the marina manager refused permission, outlining perceived issues with dog passports and a host of excuses surrounding red tape; I do not think he really wanted dogs in his territory. On the other hand, the tourist board was great, and at least I had an all-expenses-paid day out in Jersey.

Fame and fortune were to continue – Whizz received his first dog trust award on the 8th of February at the Guildhall in London, and shortly after, we were contacted by a London production company who wanted to film Whizz for a Channel 5 new series about dogs.

Initially, I was excited about this proposition; it would yield further opportunities for Ellie and Whizz. After many repeated questions and answers that seemed to go in one ear and out the other, I, along with Whizz and Ellie, met the producer at Oxwich Bay one afternoon in May. More of the same questions came thick and fast; reiteration is not really a strong enough word I had in mind. On top of this, after incessant phone calls bombarding my line the following day, along with all the same questions asked again, I decided enough was enough.

I was a little disappointed for Ellie, but Whizz wasn't bothered; there would be plenty more things going on. "Get off that phone, Dave. Give it a rest and take me for a walk!"

Disappointment did not last long, and it was only a matter of weeks when the BBC contacted regarding the proposed One Show shoot, and efficiency erupted in abundance. Therefore, it was on a warm summer's day in July, off we went to our favorite Oxwich Bay to film with Clare Balding and the crew. This was a truly golden opportunity to promote not only our charity but also the work of the Swansea Marine Volunteers, of which Whizz was a fully-fledged member.

The filming went like clockwork, and I was pleased that the producers respected my thoughts on the best shots of the 'rescues' in the calm bay. Clare interviewed Ellie on the bobbing boat and also me on the shore line. The pair were superb, and, much to the delight of all concerned, the whole project was done and dusted in a couple of hours.

The schedule for the recordings airing on the 'One Show' was not until mid-November – we were in the hands of producers on that one, but the week prior to this, we were contacted and invited to talk with them on the day of the broadcast, live on the show. At first, they were a little reluctant to have young Ellie there; that was not an option as far as I was concerned; we were a team.

Ellie was highly delighted, especially as she was able to skip school early. With her father, Adam, glued to the SATNAV, we set off on a gloomy mid-November evening. M4 and rush hour? – bad enough. Finding a new television centre? It would have been easier thrashing through unmarked territory in the Amazon rainforest armed with a blunt machete.

I think it was pure luck that we turned down a side road into what looked like an industrial estate. Stopped by guards and interrogated, it did appear we were in the correct place, and we were directed to a small door leading to some sort of office block. This was a far cry from the old BBC studio I knew.

Adam and Ellie went into the building to sort things out whilst I stayed with Whizz, who, by then, needed to do what dogs need to do. No way would I risk that with all the cables and electrical equipment inside...that would definitely be Whizz the Fizz. Also, there was the temperature issue; Whizz, with his massive furry coat, would not sustain any length of time under the heat of the lighting.

I just sat in the van waiting, which was great as to who should emerge from the building. Jeremy Clarkson and

Richard Hammond, fresh from filming Top Gear. I did not speak to them, but it was good to glimpse their famous faces; Adam was sorry to have missed them.

The main guest on the show was actor Sanjeev Bhaskar, who arrived in a large, black limousine and was ushered off inside. We met the other guests in the green room, the 'waiting' area, where we were treated to drinks and snacks.

George McGavin, an entomologist and the shows insect expert, was delightful. He made a huge fuss about Whizz, and we had a very interesting conversation about the problems of ticks and the pros and cons of different remedies on the market.

The other guest, Joe Inglis, a vet and TV personality, there to cover in case of queries and complaints regarding the arrival of a dog on live TV, was not so 'delightful' in my eyes. Whizz took a dislike to the sound engineer fiddling with a microphone on my shirt and gave a little growl. Apparently, according to Mr. Inglis, this was not a characteristic of a Newfoundland, and maybe Whizz was a dangerous dog!

Unfortunately, Ellie had to sit next to him on the red sofa, but also with a more pleasant human being – the actor Sanjeev Bhaskar. I was seated beside her with Whizz, Adrian Chiles, and Christine Bleakley (now Lampard).

The session was a major accomplishment. Whizz behaved impeccably and gazed at himself contently on the big screen. Ellie proved her abilities beyond well, and her interview with Clare Balding was brilliant. Adrian and Christine loved Whizz, and there was a great deal of talk and interest taking place on and off the screen. The vet, however, once the interviews were over, seemed to make a sharp exit!

What a great experience for young Ellie, a star, on TV, with all her school pals watching at home; I was very proud of both of them.

Opportunities flooded in after the One Show; it was the start of a number of TV appearances – it seemed we were famous!

One of the best invites was the chance to be involved at Maidstone studios for the filming of 'Sports Relief Top Dog', an experience I knew Ellie would enjoy. Packed with fun games, it was a chance to meet more celebrities as they took part with their dogs, competing against two members of the public and their pets. It was to be a ten-day marathon of recording, to produce fifteen episodes, and I had the task of coming up with fifteen games to go with them!

I was very pleased to be asked for my advice, and myself and Ellie were put in charge of the swimming sessions. Our expertise, not only in the coaching of swimming dogs but also in health and safety, were greatly valued. A huge indoor pool was constructed, with a raised stage at one end; quite alien to us, but a good design for our doggie friends.

Ellie was in her 'Elliement', meeting all sorts of famous people. Bob Geldof's daughter, Peaches, became quite a friend, and there was quite a bond between them. Peaches had recently put a deposit on a Newfoundland puppy a few weeks before the show, and Ellie gave her some good advice.

Such was their friendship that Peaches was keen to bring the puppy to our training sessions once it was old enough. Tragically, before this could happen, Peaches died of an overdose which certainly had an effect on Ellie. What a terrible thing to happen and a waste of a young person's life.

The time spent at Maidstone was amazing for Ellie, but not all quite 'hunky-dory', as she found out to her detriment.

The BBC auditioned all the contestants well before filming at Maidstone studios from all over the UK, asking them to show off their dog's abilities to the producers of the show. For practical reasons, the swimming capabilities could not be properly assessed until they arrived with us at the pool in the studio. I asked producers to tell the dog owners to bring them a toy they would enjoy being retrieved from the water.

I suppose you always 'get one', don't you? A Stafford bull terrier was having none of it. Temptations by Ellie proved useless; even the dog's favorite white bowl held no interest in its enthusiasm for liquid delight. After much patience and fruitless encouragement, it was decided not a sixteen-ounce T-bone steak smothered in peanut butter was going to entice it into the depths. Sadly, the contestant had to be sent home with apologies, chocolates, and flowers.

The internet trolls that attacked Ellie the next day were disgusting, to say the least. A massive number of nasty messages from Staffordshire terrier owners were thrust onto her Facebook page. Totally uncalled for and upsetting, particularly as the whole thing was done for charity. Thankfully the BBC and its legal team immediately stepped in and had the postings taken down within hours. I will never understand some humans at all.

For Ellie, the association with Whizz and Newfound Friends from the tender age of eleven has given her more experience and opportunities than anyone could dream of. Her loveable Whizz, her friend who helped her to overcome her fears and build her self-esteem to mountain highs.

She has since progressed through her A levels and streaked through a course at Bristol University to gain her veterinary nurse qualifications. Following the completion of her degree, she is now at Lincoln University, studying animal behavior. Fortunately, she had no problems enrolling, as I put her in touch with a good friend, Celia Haddon. A former journalist with the Daily Telegraph and a graduator of the same course at age seventy-four, she was able to give Ellie invaluable advice. I had no doubt that Ellie would excel in that, also.

Ellie is not part of my family or related in any way, but at times in your life, you see somebody times in people that you admire. I can in my own life equate to these and the people that have helped me in life. One man stood out for me, and his name was Mr. Northover, a rather wealthy gentleman with fingers in 'lots of pies'. I had to make a large oak table for him in the very early days of my career. For some reason, we had an instant bond, as was with Ellie and me.

After emerging from an award-winning apprenticeship, achieved under an unsavoury character named Victor Capaldi, I was a little cocky and high-headed. I certainly came down with a massive bump when I entered into the real business world and realized I was not, after all, Mr. Chippendale of Bristol. Mr. Northover put me on the straight and narrow, nurturing me every step of the way, and he became a life-long friend. Even with his passing ten years ago, the family friendships have not wavered; his son now being my trusted solicitor.

Maybe my gratefulness to Mr. Northover influenced the relationship I have with Ellie. We all need help in our lives, and it is wonderful to be able to do the same thing for someone else.

Ellie is on top of the world at the moment, and that is fantastic. She has achieved her goals with determination and hard work, and her success is well deserved. However, we must never forget those that have facilitated that success and be aware that life can sometimes be tough and bring you back to earth – which, in my mind, is a good thing!

Ellie Bedford and Whizz to the rescue at Oxwich Bay
South Wales

Chapter Fourteen: The Bridge

Little Bridge House is a hospice in North Somerset which was founded in 1995 by two ladies, Jo Hearn and Jill Farwell. People united in tragic circumstances, Jo having one terminally ill child and Jill with two, all needing twenty-four-hour care, they became good friends. The only respite care available for the families at the time was at Helen and Douglas House in Oxfordshire. Whilst this was a wonderful place, it was a long journey for Jo but even more arduous for Jill.

Jean met Jo at her church and was extremely moved by the talk given by this wonderful lady. The description of the vision that Jo and Jill gave of their dream to establish a hospice in the southwest was such that it touched all our hearts.

In the year 1990, these two amazing people set about fundraising in a massive way. Kitchen tables became offices; calendars were rapidly filled – without a thought for themselves, they set about striving to meet their goal. The task was huge; buildings do not come cheap, and the cost would be astronomical, but these ladies were determined to succeed. Newfound friends joined their cause the following year, and it was our charity's greatest pleasure to help. They soon became the main beneficiary of our fund-raising efforts.

Many events were held for the cause, particularly at Portishead Marina, near Bristol, where Whizz was always the star, soaring through the air and delighting the crowds as he carried out his water rescues. Our charity had good contacts, and our allies became involved in the project and were eager to help, including the organizers of The Matthew 1997 re-enactment celebrations of the discovery of Newfoundland by John Cabot.

Our close friend, Anne Mainman, a well-established artist in her own right, famous for her numerous paintings of Newfoundland dogs, sold limited edition prints and cards, and raised thousands of pounds for the cause. Everyone pitched in, with exciting water displays to grand dances – every conceivable way was explored, and the determination to succeed grew stronger with each passing month.

I am very proud to say we travelled the journey with these two incredible ladies, and in that glorious year of 1995, Little Bridge House became a reality.

Sadly, Jill's children passed away in 2004, and shortly afterwards, Jill followed in their footsteps. A memorial service was held at Exeter Cathedral, attended by admirers far and wide. The whole building was crammed with people wanting to pay their respects to this wonderful person, held in such high esteem.

After losing her friend, Jo found herself a teaching position at a private school in Kent and moved there with her husband. Tragedy was not restricted to the bereavement of the passing of her child, and we very sadly heard that her eldest son had died in a car crash in Spain. Life does not seem fair sometimes; it is difficult to understand why some families are stricken with more than their share of grief, but I will always look up to these two saviours.

Since the establishment of Little Bridge House, Newfound friends have continued to support this worthy cause, and if we can harness any support from anybody or anything, we do it. Money, of course, is the ultimate objective, but also moral support, and anything we can do to make these children and their family's lives that little better, if only for a while, is a reward in itself.

The dogs have always played a large part in that, and their visits were always welcomed by all. How could you not be cheered, cuddling up to a mass of fur, and feeling the love and compassion of a canine companion? Ted was an asset – most of the time, not so much in the water, but the children all adored his excitable and boisterous character.

I say most of the time, as there were occasions when Ted overstepped the mark with adults. I remember one occasion when he met Carol Vorderman, a neighbor, and supporter of Newfound Friends. Carol is an extremely lovely person and quite attractive – an attribute that Ted obviously found irresistible and smothered her with adoration, literally; – much to the delight of the press.

However, light-heartedness put aside, a hospice, being the caring place that it is, provides, amongst respite, palliative care. There is no getting away from the somber reality of the situation, and, in fact, that is the whole point of the charity. It is inevitably sad that solemn days were only too frequent, and although Ted was amazing with the children, on occasions, his high spirits would not be appropriate.

It was on one of these days that I was so proud of all the work our charity had done – and Whizz? Well, my heart could have burst open with pride...

Whizz jumped out of the van and sniffed the salty air. I slotted on his lead while his tail thwacked against my legs in excitement, yanking me almost off my feet towards the exit of the car park as if sensing the North Devon seaside was just around the corner.

"Sorry, Whizz," I murmured. "Not today."

I had given him a bath the night before and brushed his shaggy coat to perfection; there was no way I was going to waste all that work with a dip in the Taw Estuary.

Still, we were early and had time to stretch our legs, so I let Whizz tug me out of the grounds of the children's hospice and onto a pleasant path between trees and through the back streets of the peaceful neighborhood on the outskirts of Barnstaple. While he ambled joyfully ahead in the June sunshine, poking his nose into thickets and spritzing tree trunks where other dogs have passed. I watched him with glazed eyes, my mind elsewhere.

In my pocket was a folded letter from my vet confirming that Whizz carried no infections or intestinal worms that could cause harm to the children in the hospice. I rubbed it between my fingers anxiously as I mulled over what I was going to say to sixteen-year-old Christian and his parents.

What could I say? What does anyone say to a child who is about to die? I did not know, and not knowing was making my chest ache.

Jean and I knew the Edwards family well. We had met them at the grand opening of Little Bridge House. Christian was only four then, a little boy in a pirate bandana, face-painted beard, and moustache, who came bounding up to our dog Harry. Newfound friends had helped to fund a pirate play ship in the hospice grounds, and there were lots of other boisterous buccaneers wandering around on the open day.

Most of the would-be Jack Sparrows were a little less brave than the on-screen hero, hesitant in coming close to our enormous black and white dog with his mighty paws and lolling tongue. It was one of the reasons we chose these particular Landseers, with their panda-like features, a tad less intimidating than the all-black breed – or so we thought.

Not Christian, who, quite frankly, would not have been bothered if Whizz was blue with pink spots. He was not in the least bit scared, promptly patting Harry on the head and then throwing his arms around him, oblivious to the incompatibility in size. This small boy, fearless as the invincible Captain of The Black Pearl, Christian, became besotted with Newfoundlands for the rest of his short life.

From that day on, whenever he stayed at the hospice, Christian asked the nurses when the big dogs would be coming back for another visit. He begged his mum Sheila, to take him along to all the charity days and displays that were anywhere near his home in Devon. We always made sure he had a prime spot from which to watch the dogs, who often shook their coats dry as they passed by him, sat in his wheelchair.

"Do you want us to move his chair back a bit?" I asked Sheila one day after her son had been given another soaking.

"No, no!" she laughed, "just look!"

Sure enough, Christian was in fits of giggles, loving every minute of his saturation. From that day on, we let him enjoy it all, and Sheila came to each event armed with plenty of dry towels and changes of clothes.

I am sure Christian must have begged his parents to let him have a Newfoundland dog of his own, as he certainly had a deep and special affinity with them. He became firm friends, first with Harry, then Bear, and finally, with Whizz. I know he would have made a wonderful owner if it was not for the incurable illness that cut his short life.

One day in June 2008, not long after his sixteenth birthday, the hospice rang me to say that Christian was nearing the end of his time on earth and would I bring Bear to say farewell.

"Of course, yes," I answered without hesitation, but Bear was too poorly with his cancer to make the journey.

It was then that on that fateful day, Whizz had the honor of comforting Christian in his last moments. I knew that this young boy would be happy with my choice and, secretly, that in any event, Whizz was, indeed, his favorite Newfoundland.

I looked at my watch; it was almost time. "Whizz; let's go."

My dog looked over at me briefly, then returned his focus to a squirrel at the base of a nearby tree. I could see he was agitated, torn between loyalties. I have no idea what it is with dogs and squirrels, but these creatures, with their bushy tails bobbing madly as they scurry swiftly about their business, seem to fascinate even the very best of well-trained canines.

Normally, I would just leave him to the chase. I have never known this great lolloping mass to outwit such an adept road runner; there was no contest. Today, however, was different, and I was conscious of our appointment. I wanted to arrive exactly on time, not too early, not too late; bang on the minute, for the love of Christian.

"Oh, look!" Whizz stared up at the branches as the squirrel disappeared into the foliage. "He's climbing a tree, Dave. I think I'll just sit here and wait until he comes back down!"

"Come on, Whizz, let's go!" I repeated.

Sensing the unfamiliar tone of my voice, Whizz turned towards me, then, with one last glance towards his camouflaged playmate, left the poor animal in peace.

Over the course of my life, I had bid farewell to many a beloved family dog, but I had only seen two people slip away. My mother passed with me by her side in a hospital bed after a long battle with cancer. When someone you love is in so much pain, and you cannot do anything, it hurts so much the grief is unbearable, but I was relieved at the end when she was no longer suffering. I was only in my late twenties and wished I could have spent more time with her, but it was not to be.

Another time, a man died in my arms after his car plunged off the motorway. It was one July evening in the late nineties when I was driving home on the M4 with the dogs in the back of the van. His car suddenly appeared from the fast lane, careering across my path, and somersaulted over the barrier into a deep verge, landing upside down. I crunched to a halt, ran to his rescue, and managed to pull him out before his car burst into flames. He was still alive but sadly died before the ambulance arrived.

It was an odd thing to notice, considering the trauma at the time that the man wore no shoes or socks. I had to attend the inquest, and as it turned out, he was originally from Jordan and had recently arrived in the UK on a long flight from New Zealand. It was surmised that his feet must have swollen, hence the lack of footwear, and he had fallen asleep at the wheel.

I remember the sorrow in the eyes of his family, who thanked me, asking if any final words were spoken. I was greatly saddened that I could not comfort them; the man was completely silent, save for a very faint throbbing of a failing pulse.

I tried to redirect my thoughts as we arrived at Bridge House. It is a beautiful, honey-colored stone building tucked away on peaceful grounds in a residential area. If it were not for the welcome desk on the right, as you walk in, you would think you were in a family home, which, in many ways, it was.

The receptionist greeted us warmly and asked us to take a seat while she called for one of the nurses. Presently, a young woman arrived and led us through to a special room on the ground floor. She knocked lightly, then pushed open the door. There was Christian, lying in bed, eyes closed, his mum and dad sitting to one side, holding his hand tightly.

A skylight let in mellow sunshine, yet it was not so bright you could not see the little, starry electric lights dancing on the ceiling or the candles flickering on the shelf. Fresh flowers brightened the corners of the room, and there was a feeling of total calm and peace.

Whizz and I hovered awkwardly in the doorway. I cannot describe my emotions; I felt intrusive, and Whizz stood patiently waiting for instructions as I battled with a hint of reluctance to move forward.

"Hello," I croaked. "Are you sure you want me here?"

I had broken the silence; Christian's eyes opened, and a beaming smile spread across his face – I caught my breath. Everything brightened with that smile, and just like that, the dull ache in my chest was gone, and any feeling of alienation disappeared.

Christian's father walked over to us and reassured us that we were there for his son's wishes. He had arranged a seat on the other side of the bed, and I was aware of the slack in Whizz's lead as I led him over and unhooked his collar.

Whizz knew – he knew exactly what the situation was. My big, strong, wilful dog had the power to leap off a moving boat and tow ten people to safety, whose wagging tail could knock over a small child. My big, strong, wilful dog, who could drag me on a walk and refuse to come back until he had watched a squirrel scamper up a tree, padded noiselessly across the room, and sat calmly at Christian's bedside. Boy and dog locked eyes, and Christian reached out his frail hand, smoothing Whizz's glossy black head.

That is when I stopped worrying about what I was going to say to Christian and his parents – no words were necessary at all.

Whizz sank gently to the floor. The adjustable bed was low, and Christian was able to let his arms dangle over the edge allowing his hand to sink into the dog's warm fur. I do not exactly know how long they stayed like that – maybe fifteen minutes or so, but I know Christian was still touching Whizz when our tears began to fall as we saw the youngster pass away.

I can only think he had been waiting for Whizz to arrive, and once his Newfie friend was by his side, he was ready to move on.

There is a famous anonymous poem that tells how, when pets come to the end of their lives; they go to a place called Rainbow Bridge. All the animals who have been old, ill, and in pain are restored to health, allowing them to run free and play together in the fields, waiting for the day when they can be reunited with their owners. The Rainbow Bridge beams its prism of colour across the meadow, welcoming reconciliation and inviting man and his companion to make the crossing together.

I am not ready for that bridge just yet, but I sometimes wish Bear and Whizz had crossed it without me. I would like to think they took their place on either side of Christian, allowing his hands to furrow deep within their coats. I would like to think they crossed that bridge together, and they are there, in that wonderland, splashing in the sea, giving Christian a proper soaking, making him laugh and laugh – I really hope so...

Bear with David on a visit to the Children's Hospice Little Bridge House.

Chapter Fifteen: Be Prepared

"Be Prepared", the infamous motto of Scouts worldwide, was foremost in my thoughts as Whizz and I headed to the capital city for Newfound Friends' first London charity event for Guide Dogs for the Blind. As meticulous as my planning was on these occasions, nothing could have prepared me for the events that were about to unfold.

Nick Hardy, the head of fundraising, was the type of fundraiser that I like to work with: friendly, passionate about his charity, and showed a real interest in Newfound Friends. He had taken the trouble to travel down to London the previous year to see how we operated our charity days and was suitably impressed. "That was quite something!" he commented as we chatted after the event, "This would be amazing if we could hold a similar day in London." I totally agreed, but where at this point in time, I did not know.

I quickly ruled out The Serpentine Lake at Hyde Park, where Newfound Friends had previously been invited to star in a promotional film for The Royal Life Saving Society alongside David Hasselhoff: a great location, but with very stringent restrictions. However, a very determined Nick was on the case and rang me with great enthusiasm to tell me that the City of London River Police had suggested a potentially great location, the Docklands Scout Project, East London: an area of the Thames used for training police officers in water rescue and diving.

Not wanting to miss out on this opportunity, Nick, who seemed just as impatient as I am when it came to sorting things out, had booked a date for the two of us to assess this location. As a proper country bumpkin, the wonderful sites of London took my breath away as I made my way through the capital.

The prestigious tower blocks of Canary Wharf, home to all the major banking institutions, formed the most amazing backdrop to the Scout's Project. This really is a fantastic location, I thought to myself, and I could see from the smile that crossed Nick's face that he was feeling the same. This was before we discovered that the Scout's Project had their very own ship docked there, The Lord Amory. It was like a first-class hotel for Scouts, not like the dilapidated scout huts that I can remember from my childhood. Pure luxury, boasting its' own bar, too; definitely one of London's best-kept secrets.

Date and location set, Nick eagerly set about recruiting participants, which, with all the footage and photos he took in Southampton, I was pretty sure he would have his supporters chomping at the bit.

In the blink of an eye, a very busy July was upon us, and we were blessed with a weekend of beautiful sunshine for our trip to London. Newfound Friends had been invited to spend the night onboard The Lord Amory before our event, which was a treat in itself and guaranteed an early start the next morning.

Van packed to the rafters; the Newfound Friends boat hooked up, ready to be towed from the countryside into the city; it definitely felt like we were going away for the duration. Towing the boat through London was an interesting experience. I think people were used to seeing crafts on the Thames, not stuck in the traffic. Definitely not for the faint-hearted, but we arrived safely and were greeted by our very excited team, and it was straight down to business.

Having launched our boat in readiness for our charity day, Whizz and I desperately needed to stretch our legs and settle down for the night. As much as I would have loved to experience a luxury cabin on board the ship, my shelter for the night was under a gazebo put up around the open door of my van in which Whizz was soundly sleeping. I never like to keep any dog by itself overnight, and if it was good enough for Whizz, it was good enough for me too.

Waking to the sun rising over the tall buildings surrounding London's Docklands was surreal: an air of calmness before the storm of activity prevailed.

The Newfound Friends team was ready around 10 am, and the dogs were visibly excited by the sight of the water. The first participants, ready in their wetsuits, having had their health and safety briefing, were eyeing up which Newfoundland they would like to be rescued by. The air was filled with excitement and nervous anticipation as participants got ready to experience the power of our fantastic dogs.

Whizz was first in the boat to rescue the first participant of the day. I could hear her children telling her not to belly flop, which made me chuckle. I knew Whizz would set the pattern for the day, and I knew he would not be fazed by the new surroundings. Moreover, if Whizz was happy, the rest of the dog team would follow suit. To my delight, all the dogs performed really well, and Whizz, in particular, was flying in the new surroundings. We took the opportunity to film Whizz in action during the day, and such was the way we took to the docklands; the film was for a very special occasion years later.

A triumphant day over, it was time to pack up and set off on our way back home to the southwest. I was feeling the effects of a lack of sleep, and Whizz was also exhausted. Arriving back home to North Somerset late into the evening, Whizz was ready for a well-deserved meal and nice rest, sleeping in his favorite spot – the back courtyard as it was a nice warm summer's evening. There was no chance of a lie-in, as I was up bright and early on Monday for my usual early morning walk before heading to my joinery workshop in Bristol.

Even now, I am still coming to terms with the events that followed our charity day. Life is often described as a rollercoaster ride, and over the next few days and weeks, our ride reached depths that I did not know were possible.

As soon as I set foot into my kitchen on a Tuesday morning, it was clear to me that Whizz was not his normal self, looking very lethargic and surrounded by little piles of vomit around the kitchen floor. Whizz did not want to stand; something was dreadfully wrong. Limply, he lay there, struggling to lift his head as he looked at me with sadness in his eyes... 'Please help me, Dave.'

There was no hesitation. I needed to get Whizz to the vet immediately. I managed to encourage him to walk to my van, lifting him and driving with urgency to the vet, which was about a quarter of an hour away.

The vet's first reaction was not good and extremely worrying for me. She logged onto her computer to look up Whizz's medical record which revealed that apart from his annual vaccinations, nothing else was recorded as Whizz had been in perfect health.

The vet decided to take Whizz into their surgery in the rear of the building and put drip feeds into his legs. "Let's see if Whizz improves in a few hours", she said in a calm manner as though trying to offer me some comfort, "we will keep him here and let you know of his progress".

Very reluctantly, feeling sick to my very core, I left Whizz at the vet's and made my way back home in a daze. Obviously, I was in no mood to go to work. I phoned Frank, my business partner, to let him know. He was more than just a work colleague; he was my best friend and knew only too well how I felt about my dogs and Whizz, in particular. Pacing the kitchen, I eagerly awaited a telephone call with the hope Whizz had responded to the treatment and a, with a few tablets, I could bring him back home to where he belonged. I never like leaving any of my dogs in a place they do not know.

After an extremely long two hours, I eventually received a phone call from the vet. I was prepared for the worst possible news, but at the same time was hoping that there might be a ray of sunshine to cast over my gloomy mood. Whizz was hanging on but not responding to treatment. The vet told me that she, herself, could do no more and asked how I would feel if she made arrangements for Whizz to be admitted to a veterinary hospital. I did not need to ask twice, and whatever it was going to take, I wanted Whizz to get the very best medical attention.

Bristol University has a good veterinary school in Langford, on the outskirts of the city. It has a fantastic reputation, and that is where Whizz and I were heading. I had not any previous dealings with them, but I knew people in the dog world have always spoken highly about their expertise. Arriving at the security gates, it felt like an eternity before the security guard confirmed I had an appointment. I felt myself getting cross. I could feel my face burning as I was so very anxious to get Whizz to their surgery for immediate attention and care. Fortunately, once I got the green light, three nurses awaited to help me take Whizz straight into the consulting room. They very kindly asked me to leave Whizz in their care. With a heavy heart, I kissed Whizz on his face, not sure if I would never see him alive again.

Upon leaving, I was asked to sign a number of papers, mainly to show I was in a financially stable place to pay for

Whizz's treatment. I would have willingly signed up to join the Foreign Legion if it would make Whizz better; such was my emotional state. I was given various telephone numbers and times to call to find out about Whizz's condition. If the worst came to the worst, I wanted to know straight away and made that very clear to the vet who came to see me after Whizz's admission to the hospital. With this agreement in place, I was told to go home as there was nothing more I could do for Whizz, and I was assured that he was in the best possible place.

I did not sleep well at all that night, and I could not help thinking that I had seen Whizz for the last time. Exhausted, I made the dreaded phone call to Langford hospital promptly at 9 am. Although Natasha was busy and unable to talk, I was informed that Whizz had made it through the night and his condition was unchanged. Hearing those words was a huge relief; the more time Whizz was able to fight his illness, the more time it gave the experts to get to the bottom of the cause of his condition. I asked if I could visit Whizz later in the day; I was desperate to see my best friend. To my delight, it was confirmed that it was possible at an arranged time of 3 pm.

There was nothing more I could do but live in the hope that Whizz would pull through, get better and be back to his normal self. So, with this positive thought, I went back to work with the expectation that keeping busy might just be the best thing for me. Whizz was never far from my thoughts, and every time my phone rang, there was a nervous wait to hear from whom the call was from.

All my friends knew just how I was feeling and expressed their hope that Whizz would pull through. The team of Newfound Friends asked if we should cancel the charity event for the coming Saturday. In true fighting spirit, I told my team that we would go ahead. It takes many months for charities to organize and prepare their supporters taking part in these events, and there is a huge amount of money resting on these days.

Saturday's charity day was to be held at Watermead Lake, Aylesbury, in aid of Dogs for Disabled People. Just before Whizz was taken ill, the charity called to say they had their full quota of people taking part (thirty participants), and, of those, several of them disabled people themselves.

Newfound Friends always love to give disadvantaged people the opportunity to experience the strength and power of our dogs in the water. On such occasions, additional effort and members are needed in the Newfound Friends team to keep disadvantaged people safe in the water. Whizz would have wanted the day to go ahead, I was sure, so we agreed to keep our promise for our charity beneficiaries and honor their special day. It was perfectly clear that whatever happened with Whizz, and with such a full calendar year ahead, Whizz would not be able to take his place in the team. A bitter pill to swallow.

Whizz's illness brought about young Ted's opportunity to fill in for Whizz, and whilst he would never be able to fill Whizz's shoes, he would do his best for his brother. Ted lived very much in Whizz's shadow as Whizz was impossible to match as a swimming dog. Ted swam well with a great top line in the water, which is always a great sign I like to see in our dogs. When the rear end of a dog goes under the water, it's a sign that the dog is struggling or tired. This was never the case with Ted, naughty as he still was on land, and although not anywhere near as fast as Whizz, he was a 'Steady Eddie' in the water.

I remember on one of Ted's early days of training, he set off across the lake, swimming the full width of half a mile. I called him back to the shore, but in true Newfoundland fashion, Ted decided to exert selective hearing and, in Terrible Ted fashion, chose to completely ignore me. Knowing I wanted him to return, he decided in his infinite wisdom, 'Oh no, I could not really give a toss what Dave wants. I am going for a nice swim!' We ended up driving around the circumference to pick Ted up and return him to base. That's Ted to a 'T', always a character with his own mindset, but never to be a Whizz.

Yet, Ted did his brother proud, and as it became obvious that Whizz was going to be confined for a while, there were more events to be tackled; Ted sprang into action, as usual, in more ways than one.

The Isle of Wight annual charity event due to take place the following week at the world-famous pub, The Folly, was always a superb event, arranged well in advance - and Whizz was booked for a starring role. It was a major operation for the team, involving expensive ferry crossings of two hundred pounds plus. Thankfully, the hospice was able to obtain free tickets for us, which made it infinitely more exciting.

Leaving Whizz was heart-breaking, but Jean was on hand with daily visits and updates; I, therefore, concentrated on the festival and, of course, Ted.

The previous year's camping palaver was disastrous, raining cats and dogs. There was more water on the site than at the actual event. Thus, I decided to book a lovely holiday let, set in the town of Ventnor, within Fort Victoria, a Napoleonic historic estate. Quite small, with only one room, it was stunningly designed with a magnificent arched roof and ornate woodwork...How fabulous was that? – and how fabulous was the temptation for Ted!

It was only luck that I managed to procure the services of a local joiner, who came to my rescue to put right the chewed-up, mangled, wooden mess of the patio doors before anyone found out. Good old Ted, but how could you be cross for long when I was frantic about Whizz and the young Newfie was doing his best to keep up the high standards of his brother in the water...Oh Ted, what to do with you?

A new routine was established with Whizz in the hospital. Each day I would travel to Langford Hospital to see Whizz and would always call first thing each morning for updates and news of any diagnosis. There was little change in his condition, and whilst it was good that he was hanging on to life, he was not getting any better. I was completely baffled, and as each day passed, my frustrations grew. As hard as it was at times, I never gave up hope.

The weekend of our charity day was upon us, which brought about the hundred-and-ten-mile trip to Aylesbury, setting off with Ted and towing our boat at 6 am. This was far too early to call the hospital, so I decided to wait until our arrival at Aylesbury and call then. Natasha was on leave over the weekend, and I was put through to the vet to cover for her.

From the moment the conversation started, it was frustratingly clear that I would not understand a word the male vet was saying. Bristol University is renowned for its excellent educational and treatment facilities, and consequently, many overseas applicants apply for their courses. I am sure this gentleman was much better educated than myself, but his command of the English language was, in a word, abysmal. I just could not even grasp the gist of the conversation and cut short the call as politely as possible. On putting the phone down, I rang the receptionist at the hospital again, explaining I needed to find out how Whizz was and asked if she would call me back with an update on his condition.

When you have an animal in a serious condition, you want to know, above all else, how they are doing. It caused me great distress when I could not find out any information – you fear the worst. Fortunately, I received a call a little later from Langford to say Whizz had a comfortable night but with little change.

Despite my low mood, the charity day was brilliant, with many happy and excited participants raising tens of thousands for Dogs for Disabled People. Ted was well-behaved; (well, as best he could be!) and performed well, but as much as I love all my dogs, I could not help but think, 'it should be Whizz here today.'

By the time Ted and I got back home, it was far too late to visit Whizz. I could not bear the thought of another difficult phone call, so I reluctantly decided to wait until Sunday morning to make contact with Langford again. Although exhausted, it was another sleepless night.

The daily phone calls and visits to see Whizz continued for twenty long days. Each and every day, I was given a different diagnosis and varying prognoses. In total, I counted twenty-seven things Whizz could be infected by; YES, TWENTY-SEVEN! Confusing and beyond belief, I was rapidly losing faith; would my Whizz ever come out of this? I felt drained trying to make sense of it all... From my analysis, I could detect some common ground. Liver failure came to the fore on a few of the possible ailments, but nothing more was considered on that front. Samples were sent to European experts for investigation, and no stone seemed to be left unturned in trying to get to the bottom of Whizz's illness. Whizz was holding his own, but I think the drugs they administered helped to keep a very strong and giant dog subdued. Heart-breaking to witness a dog of great strength become so weak.

Then, we had a miraculous breakthrough – one of our European friends asked if anyone had considered that Whizz might be infected by leptospirosis. I did not know whether to be uplifted, that we may, after all, get to the bottom of the problems, or devastated to hear that word. Leptospirosis is an extremely serious infection, spread by rat urine, frequently in rivers and lakes – and in nearly all cases, it is fatal. The name sent shivers down my spine.

However, that 'thought' by our friend undoubtedly saved Whizz's life. An urgent test for Leptospirosis was carried out, the results confirming that, indeed, it was the cause of Whizz's condition. Immediately Whizz was given the correct medication, and whilst the effects took time to make a difference, within a few days, there were signs of a steady improvement.

Whizz continued to progress daily, and I could see my dear friend getting back to his normal self, very much to my relief, and my prayers answered; it could have so easily gone the other way. Over the next few days, Whizz's condition got so much better, and I was allowed to walk Whizz on the grounds of the hospital. I do not know what he felt about being closely followed by a nurse armed with a bucket of disinfectant, which she promptly chucked over any spot that Whizz cocked his leg on, but I think he was just grateful to be back on his feet. Leptospirosis is highly infectious, and Whizz was immediately placed into quarantine away from all the other kennelled dogs – A little too late, I thought, as Whizz was with all the other dogs in the care of the hospital for nearly three weeks!

Against all odds, Whizz made a full recovery, which goes to show his strength and determination to succeed. I thank God for giving him back to us, but questions had to be asked. After the huge relief of discovering what was wrong with Whizz and seeing him cured and back to his normal self at home, my gratefulness turned to anger – I wanted answers. Why did Whizz have to suffer for so long? Why were we put through so much stress and anxiety? Why wasn't Whizz protected by his annual injections?

Whizz always had his annual vaccinations, something I consider so very important for a swimming dog. Leptospirosis is one of the diseases these injections give immunity against, the most common infections dogs might pick up. Whizz's medical records showed he had been vaccinated against this awful disease, so, understandably, the thought that Whizz had Leptospirosis was discounted firstly by my vet and not questioned in the report she sent to Langford Hospital.

As soon as the diagnosis was confirmed, Natasha, Whizz's assigned vet, filed a vaccination failure report. This report was sent to the vet who administered the injection, the pharmaceutical company that supplied the vaccine, and the Royal College of Veterinary Surgeons. The failure report is investigated by the Royal College of Vets, who, as part of the process, visit the vet that administered the vaccine to see if all procedures are in order and proper care is taken with all their animal practices. Any discrepancy that they discover that is not in line with correct procedures for the welfare of animals can lead to a vet being removed from their register. Needless to say, vets do not welcome visits from the Royal College of Veterinary Surgeons as it is, in general, looked at as a black mark against their name. In short, it is, and quite rightly so, a serious business.

A well-known pharmaceutical company manufactured the vaccine administered to Whizz. From the time of a dog's first injection, each dog is issued with a booklet that is stamped after each annual vaccination. The vaccine is also recorded as to the supplier and batch number by way of a sticky tab that is stuck onto the book, dated and signed by the vet to prove the injection was carried out.

The Royal College of Vets had informed the company of the failure report sent from Bristol University Veterinary

School, highlighting the college's concerns about the vaccination report. It was within a matter of days that I received a telephone call from the pharmaceutical company, and I was immediately informed that I was speaking to their head vet employed by the company, Mr. Kevin Whelan.

Kevin expressed his delight that Whizz was on the road to making a full recovery, and, as a gesture of good faith, the company would like to contribute to the cost of Whizz's hospitalisation at the Langford Hospital. The final bill for Whizz and his stay at Langford was a whopping £12,800, and thankfully Pet Plan, our insurers, had agreed to pay with the exception of the first £100 excess within the policy, which we paid. The pharmaceutical company were prepared to pay three-quarters of the cost. The company to my mind, did not want any bad publicity, and with Whizz by now a very high-profile dog, if the news got hold of the story, it would not serve them well.

I wanted answers, straight answers. I wrote a letter to Kevin Whelan at the pharmaceutical company asking for his company's thoughts on why Whizz had been infected by leptospirosis as he, without fail, had had his annual injections that included the leptospirosis virus protection. Why was Whizz not protected?

The reply was received and presented various theories:

1: The vaccine was not transported or stored at the correct temperature: 'I can only comment on the transport and storage of the product between/within the company's facilities and can assure you that these conditions are strictly controlled'.

2: The injection was not given properly: 'I cannot comment on this, and Susan is the best person to discuss the actual administration of the vaccine with you'.

3: The vaccine was not up to the required standard, which could be the reason why Whizz was not immune from leptospirosis.

4: There is the possibility that Whizz was one of the small proportion of dogs that do not possess an adequate immune response from the vaccine.

Dog owners are all led to believe that the annual injections give protection to our dogs on a yearly basis. After investigating, it turns out that the vaccine is only ninety per cent effective, and ten per cent of dogs do not get the cover that we would expect from the vaccinations. With all my experience, it is defiantly something I was not aware of, and I am sure lots of other animal owners would not know either.

Susan, the vet I was using at the time and to whom I trusted with Whizz's welfare, was not pleased with the fact that I had written to the company concerned, who must have sent her a copy of their letter. After everything that I had gone through, I was speechless when she phoned me at work, expressing her anger that I had the audacity to write directly to the company and had not consulted her first. Well, quite honestly, I could not give a damn about her displeasure. I was reeling that I had almost lost Whizz and told her that I would be taking my dogs elsewhere in the future and would not require her services anymore. I was bitterly disappointed by the lack of her support and appreciation over circumstances that had to be reported and also the trauma that had been inflicted upon all of us.

I cannot fully understand Susan's reaction to this day. The cynic in me thinks that the veterinary practice in question might not have wanted their relationship with the pharmaceutical company damaged. It is well known that vets are gifted with free products, days out, and pleasantries from their suppliers. Who am I to speculate? I do not know the facts about the connections with this particular company but sometimes, I do wonder.

It was clear that a number of mistakes were made all around, and Whizz had to undergo a huge amount of suffering because of a missed diagnosis. The lesson to be learnt is that medical records that show that an injection has been administered do not mean the condition should company ever be discounted. As the pharmaceutical company state, 'Not all dogs or animals get immunity from the vaccine, so never take it for granted that the dog is immune'.

When something bad happens to someone you love, you always question how it happened and whether it could have been avoided. We did not even know where Whizz picked up the virus. Could it have been from our first visit to the Docklands London? Was it when we attended a charity day the week before at Corsham in Wiltshire? Or, maybe just drinking out of the horse trough in the field? It might have been just simply drinking from the garden pond (which I filled in straight away on Whizz's return home). The saying goes, you are never more than six feet away from a rat – scary stuff indeed.

There is a light at the end of the tunnel, though; I am now more prepared. I am prepared, in the knowledge of my experience, to challenge a non-diagnosis of any of my dogs, should they ever get ill like Whizz. Most dogs would not have survived Leptospirosis, but Whizz, like me, is a fighter. Strong and resilient, fresh from a triumph on the battlefield, my Newfound furry friend was ready for his next adventure.

Whizz takes off to the rescue. The photo was published in all the national newspapers in the UK

Chapter Sixteen: Whizz and Steph

It was mid-July of 2011, a year after leptospirosis. Whizz had made a full recovery and was back to his normal self, and Ted had established his position in the family – most of the time. The business was booming in my joinery company, and, being the summer months, Newfound Friends were as busy as ever.

My time was stretched, and this meant early starts and longer days. Thankfully, the early dawn made the 5 am morning dog walking bearable. Whizz was always reasonably well-behaved, and I could usually achieve the task within the limited time restraints, despite the need to meet the numerous contracts that were bombarding my business.

I say usually, but Ted? Well, you know Ted by now. He would constantly pound off into the distance, determined to do whatever he liked and to 'have a ball'. It was pretty ironic that Ted did not really possess a pair of those manly circular breeding facilitations... They were hiding, still desperate to hang on to dignity within his rapidly expanding frame. The Vet informed us Ted was perfectly healthy, and the fact that his pair of lady-killers had not dropped was not an issue at all. Whether this had an effect on his behavior was hard to tell; no ladies had actually come his way to date, and in any event, he seemed more interested in wreaking havoc everywhere else.

Whizz had regained his top-dog status as head of the team and tried to do his best by Ted, generally dealing with the unruly juvenile, by completely ignoring his escapades and looking at him with silent words... 'What a pillock!' However, sometimes, the temptation became too much, and very occasionally, I was off chasing the dastardly duo.

Much as Ted was hard work and not as agile in the water as Whizz, naughtiness was normally confined to home life. He was still a strong swimmer and involved with the training, having gradually taken over from my now age, Newfoundland 'Bear', but Whizz still retained the leading role. Ted's real expertise lay in his companionship with all the children in the hospice and, indeed, landlubbers of all ages. Loveable and friendly, that is the general character of Newfies; therefore, Ted, being no exception, successfully established his place within our family and the team but generally stuck to the 'kids'.

This particular July was hectic. My business had secured a contract to refit a restaurant at St Pierre Golf and Country Club, just over the Severn Bridge in Chepstow. It took two whole weeks to complete, and although we were supposed to finish the work on Friday, it was clear by the middle of the second week we were in danger of encroaching on the annual Swansea Yacht club race due to take place that weekend. The event was always well attended, with around forty craft competing, negotiating the course from the marina, around the Gower Peninsula, and returning to Swansea. It was essential that safety cover be provided, and it was up to the Marine Rescue team, including Whizz, to provide it.

There was leeway to finish the project, but it could have entailed penalties if it was delayed. We worked closely with Whitbread with design and provision; it was not in our interests to run over on the job. Thankfully, my foreman and one of the apprentices worked over the weekend, freeing me up to supervise the Swansea race... or so I had hoped.

Much as I would have enjoyed a relaxing weekend, it was not to be duty calls. Therefore, it was a bleary-eyed Dave that bundled Whizz and a very excitable Ted into the van at silly o'clock to make the trip to Swansea and to my Auntie Mary's house. I had no intention of taking Ted to the actual event for obvious reasons, and so my aunt had the pleasure of dog-sitting that day. Thankfully, she shares my love of dogs and is very patient; I knew Ted would be in safe hands...

Whizz, overjoyed to leave his unruly brother behind, and was enthusiastic to get on with the real work of the day. He just loved the sea, with the briny smell of the ocean infusing his dewy nostrils and the coastal winds blowing through his thick shaggy coat. The look on his face told all – "Come on, Dave, let's go!"

As we pulled into the Marina car park, I became acutely aware of something sadly amiss with the van. It veered to the right as I ground to a halt outside the headquarters of the volunteer's unit, and I knew exactly what the problem was. This is where you start cursing yourself for ignoring warning signs because you are too busy doing other things. A stitch in time did not save nine, and a repairable puncture airing its presence during the week, tyre now stuffed in the boot as a spare, was as useless as a chocolate teapot – I now had a full-blown flat pancake on the front.

Keith, our friend from the maritime rescue team, made his way over, but despite all his good intentions, rescuing me was not on the cards – AA it had to be. I am surprised it was the Automobile Association I was calling, not Alcoholics Anonymous – such were the trials of the week!

Whizz was becoming incessantly anxious to get to work in the boat. Keith suggested that the team take Whizz with them while I waited for the AA. Much as I like to be with

Whizz, I had no choice, the planned lockout was imminent, and the safety team must be at sea to safeguard the competitors.

I trust the team implicitly, and Whizz was well capable of looking after himself; I was confident he would be in safe hands. He was used to swimming with different partners, and as, for once, Ellie was not in the limelight, Stephanie, a very intelligent, experienced volunteer came on board – literally. She had worked with Whizz many times before, and I was extremely pleased that she was there to accompany my canine friend. As for Whizz, he wouldn't be bothered – as long as he was in the water, he was happy.

Steph joined the Marine Volunteers in her early teenage years, having been introduced to it by her father. From that young age, she had now blossomed into a woman in her late twenties, elegant and tall, with long blonde hair cascading over her shoulders. You could compare her to a 'Baywatch Babe', but she was so much more than the glamourous actresses of the famous TV series. Steph was, to all intense and purposes, more qualified than many of the men on the team. She held a full skipper's boat and radio license, together with the all-important first aid certificate.

Full of enthusiasm and dedication, I had always admired Steph, particularly as she had bought her own specialist wet suit to swim with Whizz; at three hundred pounds, this was no thrifty purchase.

The dry suits the volunteers normally wear are great for weather protection but not good for swimming to a rescue.

I placed Whizz's harness over his head and strapped the buckles underneath his body, telling Steph to make sure to readjust them after swimming as they tend to loosen when wet. The inflatable, 'Jack Tar', named after the nickname given to the men of Swansea, was waiting for the off, and, clutching a hand-held VHF radio, I reluctantly waved goodbye. The arrangement was to meet them all later at Oxwich Bay once the van was fixed, and this way, we could keep in touch.

The many yachts sailed majestically into the locks awaiting transference to the open waters. I marvelled at the splendour – and the expense. The small bobbing orange inflatable, so tiny in comparison but oh, so important, closely followed the troop and took its place amongst the elite.

I watched from the quayside as a final, very large vessel squeezed into the lock, just behind the volunteers – it was a tight fit and awkward to manoeuvre in a small space. I noticed it was called 'Mischief', and a brief, comical thought sprung to mind that Ted would be completely at home on a yacht that was so aptly named. I wondered how he was getting on with Auntie Mary and what 'mischief' he was up to.

All the yachts were packed in like sardines and anxious to move out. The seawater could not pour in quickly enough to gain a safe level to allow the vessels to pass through the outer lock gates and onward into the swirling waves of the Bristol Channel.

Releasing the mooring ropes slowly, the volunteers' boat moved forward. Whizz, tongue panting and tail wagging with excitement, stood near the small launch platform, specifically designed for the jump, and stared longingly out to sea. Not a glance did he have for his owner, who lovingly cared for his every need.

The three-man crew of The Mischief followed suit and began to haul in the protective mooring fenders. I could see clearly from the shore that an elderly sailor was having difficulty retrieving the fender at the rear end of the boat; it did appear it was snagged on some obstruction or other.

As with all these dreadful events, things happen in a flash of a second. One minute the crew member was tugging at the fender, the next, he had fallen head-first into the murky waters with a huge splash. The poor man had not even had the time to put on a life jacket (a lesson to be learned there), and he was totally disorientated and floundering in the drink.

He started to panic uncontrollably, and our rescue inflatable was facing the wrong way and was beginning to head out to sea amongst the sandwiched crowd of boats!

Thank goodness for the radio; there was no time to lose. I yelled into the mouthpiece to alert Keith, but Jack Tar could not turn; there was just no room! "Switch off the engine! Swim back to him!"

My alerts were certainly warranted, but I need not have shouted directions with Whizz on the team. To this day, I do not know how Whizz senses trouble, even if he cannot see it. Already he was on the case. Steph. With her immense knowledge and experience, she had instantly assessed the situation and immediately dived with Whizz; both were swimming strongly towards the casualty.

Calming the gentleman down, Steph managed to coax him into grabbing Whizz's harness and making him understand that Whizz would do the rest. Thankfully, the casualty was able to comply with the instruction, and Whizz, being Whizz, needed no telling to get on with the job and tow the man to the Jack Tar. Steph swam alongside both of them, ensuring safe passage to the rescue boat and all three were hauled into the inflatable... a rescue carried out to perfection – Well done Whizz and Steph!

The unfortunate sailor was shivering and wet but otherwise unharmed and had no indications of shock. There was no choice for both boats to move out into the channel in the first instance. Keith offered to return the grateful gentleman to shore; however, sailors being sailors, the sopping victim was determined to carry on regardless. His shipmates plied him with hot drinks and discarded his soaking clothes with new, warm attire. Soon he was just about back to normal, and Keith radioed to me that all was okay and they were going to carry on with their mission.

I made my way back to the marina car park, where the AA was eagerly waiting for my arrival. Slightly embarrassed, I explained to the patrolman all the tribulations of the week and that the spare was also flat. Good on these people, he did not condemn me at all or give me any knowing; 'Well, that serves you right for being an idiot' look. In fact, he was a magician and produced a canister of liquid gold and pumped up the offending rubber ring in minutes.

"That should be enough to get you to the local garage; they will be able to sort you out in no time," he beamed, giving me directions.

'No time' turned into four hours, as sod's law, the tyre was unrepairable, and they did not stock my size of new ones

– but all was not lost; they could order one to be delivered straight away from their warehouse. I suppose I should be grateful I was not there all night.

Undeterred and on the road again, I made my way to Oxwich Bay only to find no one there... I had the feeling it was going to be one of those weeks. Contacting Keith by radio again, it turns out another rescue had been necessary; this time, no casualty in the water, but a yacht with a broken rudder, and they were towing back to the marina.

As I arrived at the yacht club car park, my spirits were lifted as I could see Steph walking with Whizz by her side, both safe, looking very pleased and chirpy. The danger of the encounter did not enter their minds, and the beam that had spread across Steph's face told all.

The pair of them were soaking wet, unlike myself, who had, unusually, escaped any drop of the ocean. That was easily rectified when we hosed Whizz down with fresh water, flushing out all the salty brine from his heavy coat. Note to self – when in dry clothes near a big soggy dog – stand back.

Steph was thrilled to have been part of the life-saving rescue with Whizz at her side. I was incredibly proud of each- how courageous and talented they both were! It made the negative issues of the day disappear into the evening sunset as I drove my hero back to Auntie Mary's.

Tired and a little weary, I parked outside the cottage and glanced at my phone. A welcome text greeted me from Frank at St. Pierre, saying the job had been finished a day early without me. There was no message from Auntie Mary – could it be true? Dare I enter into the apocalypse?

All was strangely quiet as I left Whizz to water the flowers; I made my way tentatively through the back garden and into the conservatory – and there he was. Ted, the mischief-maker of Swansea town, was fast asleep on the tiles. Everything seemed intact, and Auntie Mary came bounding out to say what a lovely day it had been, and wasn't Ted, an absolute angel?

I refrained from replying, "I did not know Lucifer had any apprentices," and thought, maybe, just maybe, I had misjudged Ted and what an amazing day it had turned out to be, after all.

Steph and Whizz to the rescue

Chapter Seventeen: The Russian Lifeguard

The respite care for the Russian children came about shortly after Whizz arrived. My daughter Colleen had left for the University of Edinburgh, and despite the house being large enough to house half the inmates of Battersea, there was a void that needed to be filled.

Jean and I had been listening to the radio and found ourselves engrossed in the story of the children in Belarus that had been adversely affected by the Chernobyl nuclear disaster. The effects of the accident at the nuclear plant in the North of Ukraine on that fateful day in April 1986 had far-reaching effects far into Western Europe. Belarus, being positioned directly on the border, had suffered nearly three-quarters of the fallout, well past thirteen kilometers into the country.

Thus, The Chernobyl Lifeline Appeal charity were asking for help from the UK general public to offer temporary care within their homes to give the children a break from the horrors inflicted upon them.

At first, we debated whether to just donate funds from Newfound Friends, but after contacting the radio producers, we attended a meeting at a public house in Hartcliffe, on the outskirts of Bristol we changed our minds; our hearts went out to these young people, as their story evolved.

Hartcliffe is a relatively large housing estate in Bristol; notorious in its own right for all the wrong reasons; it seemed to be a strange place to hold a welfare meeting about Russian children. However, it was clear that the organising group was passionate about their cause, and a vast array of people from all walks of life and class attended, from the wealthy to the not-so; the interest was heart-warming to see.

We heard about the aftermath, we heard about the deprivation, and most of all, we heard about the plight of the children...

Belarus sometimes referred to as Bella Russia (ironically meaning 'White Russia'), is an extremely poor country. Corruption is rife, and there is little opportunity for people to succeed in life. To find employment would be a blessing, and many men (and a few women, no doubt), through depression and lack of pride in the ability to provide for their families, took to vodka to while away the days of hopelessness. The frustration, fuelled by drunkenness, inevitably raised its ugly head in the form of violence and abuse.

This inevitably takes its toll on the whole family, showing the extent of the problems in the national divorce statistics, which run at some 70%. The Chernobyl disaster only served to exacerbate the situation. You can only imagine what these people had and were going through – of course; we wanted to help!

Jean was compassionate and all for the project, as was I, though I had slight reservations about the dogs. Not that I was worried about any child's safety, the Newfoundland had been a complete asset and delight to the residents of Little Bridge House – I was more concerned about how our little visitors would take to the mob. The more I thought about it, the more my apprehension reduced, and I realized it was highly likely to be an advantage. These children needed a bit of love and kindness brought into their gloomy world.

The essential checks were carried out – no problem for us; our Newfound Friends Charity would not function without them, and the day soon arrived when we welcomed Sasha and Alan into our lives.

It was a warm summer's day in August 2007 when the coach pulled up on the seafront in Clevedon, the small coastal town near my home. The pier, in its magnificence, stretched out into the lapping waves of the ocean, holding out a welcoming hand to visitors, young and old.

Two blank faces, eyes devoid of emotion, noses squashed against the window, peered into a strange world.

Belarus is landlocked, and I doubt these young people had ever seen the sea, let alone played on sand, or even had any kind of holiday at all – it must have been so much for them to digest.

There were around forty boys on the coach in all, the girls having already been dropped off in Bristol. They all trundled down the steps and formed a group around the interpreter as each child was assigned their family and accommodation.

They all looked a little forlorn, clutching their brown paper bags containing a few essentials; it reminded me of scenes of evacuation during World War Two, when the children were sent to the countryside, away from the destruction and bombs. Was this much different? I suppose, at least, the explosion was no more.

Alan Sychesky was ten years old, thin and pale - the eldest of the two boys. Sasha Kotovich was a year or so younger – scrawny and fair-haired. These newly acquainted mini-humans looked like they hadn't had a meal in weeks. This was why they were here, in desperate need of good food, medication, and above all, some TLC, and Jean, myself, Whizz, and the rest of the doggie brigade were going to provide that, even if only for a month.

The language barrier was an issue at first; neither of us spoke Russian, and the boys not speaking English. German faired a little better; therefore, Jean, being fluent, had more success than myself. We also had a good friend, George, originally from Bulgaria, who spoke many languages and helped enormously with his frequent visits to ensure everyone was happy and content. Children soon learn to pick up different tongues, and the boys coped very well – in fact, I am sure they did not let on how much they really understood some of the time!

The boys settled in well and began to thrive in their new temporary environment. It turned out Alan needed treatment for a heart condition, and this was duly arranged by the Lifeline charity, and he received good care at the Bristol Children's Hospital. Sasha was luckier in that sense, though he had two missing fingers on his left hand, apparently chopped off on his hunt for firewood. We also found out later during that month that his sister had cancer and was unable to travel; therefore, he was not without his own issues.

And the dogs? Bear took to the children instantly, being intuitively drawn to our young friends and, even more so, those that were sick and in need; his vast experience in hospice visits saw to that one.

Izzy was a little standoffish at first, but as soon as he realized the boys were not about to nick his chicken and were, actually, quite 'alright', he became a good company. Joking aside, I would not have been surprised if the boys did pinch a treat or two. I wonder what they thought of three humongous dogs, bigger than themselves, eating more luxurious food than they had ever set eyes on?

Whizz, still young but also huge, was totally confused. 'What's going on with this then, Dave? I thought I was the new kid on the block – do these little people play or what?'

It did not take Bear long to use his psychic leadership skills in convincing Whizz that these two beings were not aliens from outer space and that all was hunky dory in the Pugh household. Soon, he was aching for his newfound buddy and formed a particular friendship with Sasha.

By the end of August, Jean and I were on our knees, utterly exhausted, looking after these two very adventurous young boys. Our free time disappeared as we partook of hospital visits, pre-arranged excursions, long walks in the countryside, and incredibly lengthy cycle rides – not really what you had envisaged after a long day's work.

The boys thrived both mentally and physically, and this was evident in their blossoming, healthy complexions and confidence. I admired them greatly in their appreciation of the freedom whilst they winged their way on two wheels, fresh air blowing in their faces as they raced along the paths. They cared not about other local children, staring and giggling as they rode upon cycles made for girls. They cared not about having the right trainers or fashionable clothes that British children seemed to expect.

Attitudes did not go without little mischievous adventures – as with any young boys would do, and in some ways, it was pleasing to see – in other ways, not...

The boys had been given cameras at the beginning of their stay to record their times with us, primarily to show their families on return. It wasn't until the photos were developed shortly before they left that the truth arose. I had been very conscious of safety for both our visitors and the dogs, ensuring the gates were locked at all times, avoiding enthusiastic escapes to ventures far and beyond, and preventing any potential thefts.

The self-esteem in both Sasha and Alan had grown to such an extent it transpired they had been on journeys, several actually, all over the village and further afield! Well, I guess they did not come to any harm – and boys will be boys, as we found out after they had left...

I did wonder what the smell was as I strolled down the path and passed the sewage manhole. It certainly was not the prize blooms, and, in any case, these were already trashed by liquid poison and heavy paws. It was definitely not the odour of dog – let's say 'waste'; we were always careful to clean up on a regular basis. There was no choice when you had three big dogs in the house, and pungent manure was of no use when you had no plants to nurture.

The dogs just sat there sniffing the air and gawping. Whizz stared into my eyes; "don't look like that. Nothing to do with us!"

There was no choice; the job had to be done. Rubber gloves and clothes-peg on the nose, the cover was heaved up, and the source of the problem was only too evident. Someone, or to be exact, some two, had taken a log from the log pile and jammed it into the drainpipe. Their maths skills were obviously not affected by their predicament – it fitted to a tee.

Hours later, with the return of fresh country air, I had a little giggle to myself. I bet those boys were laughing their new socks off, sitting on the plane, eating cake, and drinking orange juice; a far cry from when they first arrived – how could you be cross for long? It was rewarding enough that we thought the boys enjoyed their stay and became happy and healthy young chaps. It was sad to think that Alan's heart condition would only get worse, but we continued to keep in touch, supporting him from afar and sending medication to his mother.

Sasha, on the other hand, was another kettle of fish. I saw that he and Whizz formed a bond that neither Bear nor Izzie could surpass, nor they were both very sad to leave each other. I wondered if, in some way, Whizz felt some connection, sharing the disadvantaged during the first years of life.

George continued to meditate, and I asked whether Sasha could swim. Affirmation was not really the key; we never really knew when Sasha was telling the truth. Once he was settled, it was obvious our Russian friend was bright, insisting on mending all and sundry around the house; an excellent display of dexterity, considering his slight disability. Slightly cocky, he reminded me of myself when I was his age, so how could you break ties with such an intelligent and likeable person!

We decided to invite Sasha back the following summer at our own expense, and as such was the success of this visit, we continued to enjoy his presence for short stays over the next seven years.

I arranged to pick up our young friend, for his first re-visit, from Gatwick airport. Praying that the flight with

Belavia airlines, notorious for delays, would be on time, I waited with a little apprehension – would he recognise me?

Although he had to make the trip alone, Sasha had support from a pleasant lady airline employee, who accompanied him to the arrivals gate. On seeing each other, all the worries disappeared, and we greeted each other like nothing had changed – which, by the look of him, had thankfully not. A brown paper parcel, still clutched in his hands, evoked memories; happily, this time, he also possessed a small hand luggage bag.

Onwards to North Somerset, where all three dogs were anxiously waiting at the gate – it was as if they knew! Sasha was barely through the entrance when Whizz enveloped him with open paws, smothering him with sloppy licks. Bear and Izzie were more interested in the luggage. 'Were there any treats in there?'

Sasha settled in quickly and had no qualms about the house, going straight to the bedroom he had shared with Alan. It was clear Sasha still had the brightness and enthusiasm we had all come to see, and I decided to relieve Jean of daily entertainment and take him to work with me on occasion.

He was interested in the work and keen to help. Being extra careful because of his lack of fingers, I was happy to involve him in small achievable tasks; there was no way I was going to risk any accidents. Such was his enthusiasm; I could see a joiner in the making.

His friendship with Whizz could not be ignored, and I was hoping to involve Sasha with training in the water. Taking him to the leisure centre to assess his swimming ability cemented my objective; Sasha could swim – and he was a natural. Off to the lakes with Newfound Friends each Sunday, it was to be.

Whizz would look after Sasha and ensure he would come to no harm, just as he did with other children who joined in our rescue sessions. Sasha enjoyed every minute. There was no language barrier between Whizz and him, or indeed any of the dogs or the other children; it was a great way to break down any difficulties on that front. Many a photo was taken in order for Sasha to show his Russian schoolmates his escapades with the 'big dogs'.

Over the next few years, Sasha gained more experience and grew not only in lifeguard expertise but also in stature. In what seemed no time at all, and several wetsuits later, the small Russian child had matured into a young handsome, sixteen-year-old, complete with shocking bright blonde hair!

I managed to enrol Sasha in a class at the leisure centre, and he gained his bronze medal in life-saving. Together with all the lessons learned with the team, he became talented in his skills, and we were delighted to trust him, with supervision, to drive a rescue boat. He would have made an excellent Maritime volunteer, but, unfortunately, due to his nationality and his age, rules did not allow it. Sasha was bitterly disappointed.

As always, it was Whizz to the rescue, and at the tender age of sixteen, on Sasha's last holiday with us, an opportunity arose for him to come with us on a safety cover job with Newfound Friends in Bournemouth.

The day's event was to be held in aid of the British Heart Foundation – a wonderful charity that we are able to support. Bournemouth is an excellent choice for such a fund-raiser. There is a wide community of elderly residents who move into the area upon retirement and consider it a worthy cause (for obvious reasons).

No yachts were to be involved this time, but many swimmers attempted a long, sponsored swim along the whole length of the promenade, passing by three piers. It was vital that such a number of people in the water at any one time were kept safe.

We have supported you on numerous occasions at Bournemouth; however, the boat is difficult to launch, and dogs are not allowed on the beach – rescue dogs or not. It was not impossible; we had the option to take off from Poole harbor, the nearest available safe place.

It was a three-hour journey to Bournemouth; not the best when you have a boat in tow, but we made it without incident and liaised with Newfound team members Keith and Clive at Poole.

Clive was our designated driver of the day, and after the usual red tape with information to the coast guard, we were ready for the off. Sasha was excited to take part, language or no language differences; the smile on his face said it all, and Whizz was exhilarated to have his old friend on board.

There were three rescue boats altogether, placed strategically along the route. It would have been impossible for our one craft to police it all due to the limited space we were allowed to patrol outside the line of buoys protecting the participant's swimming course. We were allotted the middle slot, which was more challenging as the offshore wind was proving to be a nuisance. The boat was bobbing around randomly at times and had to be quickly tamed – much to Sasha and Whizz's amusement; they cared not one bit and were enjoying every minute. I am sure Whizz had learned a little Russian by then; he seemed to respond to Sasha's shouts with resounding barks; 'DA, DA, DA!'

The large crowd cheered as some two hundred swimmers thundered into the water – it was more like a race than a sponsored charity event, the strong 'competitors' streaking past us with no apparent difficulty. The second leg was to take place forty-five minutes later; enough time for a break.

A welcoming coffee and a bite to eat, sunning ourselves on the beach was out of the question- Whizz was banned. We made do with a jaunt into shallow waters, sufficiently low to allow Whizz out of the boat to do what doggies do... well, technically, he was not on dry land! Content we were then to partake of coffee a la thermos and a couple of squashed sandwiches.

Mid-munch, we hear on the VHF radio that the second leg of the event was delayed. Half the swimmers had not arrived and were stuck in heavy traffic – it was to be some while yet. An opportunity not to be missed, we headed for deeper waters; time for some fun in the sun and, ultimately, for Sasha to enjoy his first ocean experience with Whizz and the team.

Keith was the first to dive into the waves, closely followed by Sasha, whose exuberance beggared belief. A thumbs up from our teammate to ensure all was well with Sasha's first attempt, and Whizz was straining to be let free. Through the air, he flew like a bird and sploshed into the sea near his friend. As much as Sasha wanted to wave his arms and yell to his buddy, Gordon reminded him to lay on his back calmly, hold onto Whizz's harness, and allow a tow to the 'rescue' craft.

Sasha was well aware from our training courses that this is the desired basis for a successful recovery, and he did well to re-live the practice sessions. Although the sea can be rough, it does provide infinitely more buoyancy than inland brineless lakes, and Sasha found this task easy.

The elated expression radiating from his face was gratifying; our young Russian man was literally bathing in glory – as if all these years of marine education had come to this moment. The whole experience had been exhilarating and ultimately safe, so much so that Clive and I dived into the ocean for a relaxing swim ourselves.

The fun was to come to an end, and soon the radio was crackling again to request our return to the second run of swimmers. Joining us on board for this part of the course was a cardiologist from Southampton Hospital named Anna. As it turned out, she was to be a valuable asset to the team, as an emergency was to evolve during this second part of the day.

Regaining our position, it was clear to us all that two hundred fish were nothing compared to the four hundred mermaids and mermen preparing to tackle the course this time around. The school seemed to split into two groups; the strongest and most experienced leaping on ahead of the dawdlers, some content with a leisurely paddle along behind, others aware of pacing their stamina so as not to end up troubled. A few even gave up at the halfway point and headed back to the beach.

However hard you practice, anticipate, or underestimate your own ability, there are always unforeseen circumstances that put a strain on your health and talents. Swimming is no different; the sea and its currents can place forces upon the human body; no landlubber would understand even the most prepared and experienced can encounter great difficulties.

The lady we saw panicking close to the exclusion zone was no exception. For one reason or another, she was struggling in the water, and her head periodically disappeared beneath the surface. All hands on deck! – Whizz and the team were on the job!

Thankfully we were able to pull up relatively close to the barrier zone, where it was very clear that the situation was very serious indeed. No way could I involve Sasha in this one; without a second thought, I dived out as far as I could, with Whizz closely following on. As soon as we neared the victim, I realized the lady had become unconscious; if we did not get to her immediately, she would not survive.

All our training skills come into play in this situation. Grabbing hold of her right arm, I folded it across her body, leaving my left free to hold on to Whizz's harness. Unconscious or not, I could not take the risk of her arm lashing out, and this grip prevented any harm inflicted by such a strike. No instruction was needed from my Newfie hero – he knew exactly what to do and where to go; how strong was this animal, towing us both to safety with ease!

Once we reached the boat, Keith and Clive hauled the lady over the rubber tubes and into the rescue craft. Whizz calmly waited his turn, swimming around the boat until we could both board. Our first aid knowledge was put into practice; the lady was breathing and now semi-conscious.

Sasha was eager to help and, with no hesitation, pitched in as I instructed him to open the first aid kit and bring the foil blanket. Anna quickly placed it around the victim's shoulders and monitored the well-being of the patient, as any nurse would.

The coastguard was contacted, and Clive, having conveyed the state of the lady, was urged to make for Southbourne, at the far end of the Bournemouth beaches, towards Christchurch; St. Johns Ambulance would be waiting for us there.

The foil blanket enwrapped the victim, sufficiently warming her, stabilising her regain of consciousness, and enabling a sip of hot tea. By the time we had reached Southbourne, she was able, with a lot of help from the team, to vacate the boat, then quickly transported into the ambulance where St John took over.

Sasha stayed in the boat with Whizz, the pair of them looking slightly redundant, but much as Sasha would have liked to carry out a real-life rescue, on this occasion, the risks were too great. At least he had experienced a genuine life save, for once again, without Whizz, this lady would have surely drowned. It would be a grand story to tell on his return to Belarus. Knowing how Sasha could, to put it mildly, be frugal with the truth on occasions, I do think he would have a job convincing all his friends that he was a true lifeguard rescuer in partnership with a huge hairy dog!

A week after our day at Bournemouth, I received a telephone call from the Geordie damsel that was rescued by our shining knights. It seems she had been suffering from a nasty virus but was determined to complete the swim in honor of her husband, who had died from a heart attack the previous year. As with many a trauma, the brain blocks out the worst, and she could not remember very much about the episode. She did not remember the large shaggy Newfie towing her to the boat and was amazed to hear that it was Whizz, a trained rescue dog, who had saved her life.

Full of gratefulness and thanks, and asked if, at some point in the future if she could meet her four-legged hero. It would not have been too much of a problem as she lived on the outskirts of Southampton, easy enough for a stop off on the way to the Isle of Wight. Sadly, this was not to come about; some people would not relive such a thing, and it is totally understandable to want to forget.

Sasha was about to return to Belarus, having progressed in the UK in many ways. I was happy to offer him the opportunity to come back to Britain and, with the right work permits, forge a career in my joinery business. Money and employment were scarce in his country, and it would have been a good way of supporting his relatives, albeit from afar. I had already paid him for his labour in my business, in US dollars, as this was the easiest currency to deal in, and his family knew it was a genuine proposition, suiting us both. I had no heir that was interested in taking over the business when I retired, and I knew Sasha would, with further training, be well capable of running it. His mother and grandmother thought it was a brilliant idea. Later, Sasha must have decided otherwise; some things are not meant to be.

Saying his goodbyes to Jean, Sasha turned to the dogs, who all seemed to be aware that someone was going away. Whizz looked soulfully on when we closed the doors of the van. Sasha could only wave at his companion sadly through the window as we drove out of the cottage and onwards to Gatwick.

Armed with a new suitcase, crammed with donated clothes from many people, to take back to his family, together with a rucksack full of gifts, Sasha checked in his bag well in time for his flight. He was not allowed to take hand luggage onto the plane, but our young Russian friend was having none of it and clutched onto his treasure for dear life. It was too much trouble for the attendant to argue; he gave up in the end, and Sasha got his way.

Leaving him at the gate, he threw his arms around me, giving me a massive hug. It did cross my mind that this was unusual; Sasha rarely showed emotion but put it down to the wonderful holidays he had spent with us and the love that had grown between us all over the years. I did not realize at that time; we would never see Sasha again. This kindred spirit, this boy that we regarded as a member of our family, would be lost forever.

The days passed slowly, and Whizz remained subdued, missing his mate. Knowing Whizz, I knew he would regain his jolly demeanour shortly, though if Sasha had knocked on the door any time soon, I would be at my joinery business the next day, carving out a new one!

Jean was pottering around in the cottage and noticed that several small items, mainly Jean's jewellery, were missing. Some of the pieces had great sentimental value and could never be replaced. On further checking, I found a few personal items of mine had disappeared, along with some money. It was disappointing to deduce the culprit could not have been any other.

Sasha knew he would not be allowed back into the country without a work permit. Maybe he did not understand that I could have arranged that and taken the valuables for monetary gain. Who knows what was going on in his mind? I would like to think it was a misunderstanding, but as time passed, it became obvious that he had made a decision to remain in Belarus and avoid any further contact with us.

Neither Jean nor I bore any malice towards Sasha, and we would have welcomed him with pleasure if he were to return. We both hoped that his family, in particular his sister, well, that he had made a good life for himself and not thrown a good opportunity away.

We have since tried to find Sasha. A friend of the charity had a contact that was involved with the charity 'Surprise, Surprise'. They thought it was a fantastic story and knew I would dearly love to meet Sasha again. I am told the researchers tried very hard to find him, even travelling to Belarus with a cameraman and an interpreter. The hunt was in vain, and the only information which came to light was that Sasha had served six years in the Belarusian Army, conscription that was mandatory for all males upon reaching the age of eighteen. No one has any idea of where he is now.

All I can say is Sasha must have had his reasons; no grudge is hiding in my soul, and if ever he was to return, my open arms would welcome him unreservedly.

Sasha the Russian lifeguard

Chapter Eighteen: Oxwich Bay

"Rambo!" shrieked the sunburnt man with the three ice creams. "Rambo! Here!"

He came running awkwardly across Rhossili beach in shorts and flip-flops, holding the three cornets close to his chest with both hands. A Russell terrier bounded ahead, trailing a lead across the hot sand and making a beeline for us.

Whizz had already been harangued by one cheeky puppy that morning. Now here was another, yapping his little head off and tearing around him in crazy circuits.

"Rambo!" yelled the man, catching up with his terrier tearaway and trying to get a foothold on the trailing lead. "Leeeeeeeave it!"

By 'it', I think he meant my twelve-stone Newfoundland, though his powers of intervention were compromised by the dripping ice creams, which had probably caused him to lose control of his dog in the first place. I would have intervened myself, but Whizz didn't seem fazed.

Newfoundlands have been known to scoop up cheeky little dogs and drop them into deep water to teach them a lesson. There are newspaper reports of it happening in

Victorian times – one Newfie apparently dropped a yapping terrier into the docks and then dived straight in to rescue it! Whizz couldn't be fussed with all that; he just stood there on the sand gazing down his nose at the scrappy rascal. It was a balmy August weekend in 2008 and my Newfie's double-thick black coat, more suited to the icy waters of eastern Canada, must have felt uncomfortably warm in the Welsh sunshine.

Luckily for my hot dog, we had spent most of the morning out on the water doing what he loved best – sitting up front on the Jack Tar performing life-saving drills with the Swansea Maritime Volunteer Service (MVS). We had only come ashore to Rhossili Bay beach, on the southwest tip of the beautiful Gower Peninsula, to get some lunch and stretch our legs. Still wearing our wetsuits, unzipped, with the arms hanging free, we aimed to dry out and soak up the sunshine. Yappy little dogs, with more mouths than paws, intent on winding up our team members, were the power for the cause... Ignore them long enough; they will disappear or be retrieved by exasperated owners covered in melted ninety-nines.

It was one of those glorious Gower summer days that keep you going during the damp winters. The sky was sheer blue with just the odd fleecy cloud, and the long sweeping curve of sands below the clifftop village of Rhossili looked straight out of a glossy brochure. It was a Sunday, and dozens of families were out enjoying the sunshine, paddling in the sea and throwing Frisbees for their kids, then laughing when their dogs caught the Frisbees and cheekily absconded with their treasures.

The Welsh poet Dylan Thomas wrote of this place: 'Why don't we live here always? Always and always. Build a bloody house and live like bloody kings'. I am glad he never did build that bloody house because the unspoilt beauty of the beach is what makes it a national treasure.

Splat! Splat! In the kerfuffle of grabbing Rambo's collar, the sunburnt man had dropped two of his ice creams. He looked mournfully at the melted mess on his flip-flops and then at the steep path back up the cliff to the ice cream parlour. Poor bloke. What a flop! His kids would probably flip if he arrived empty-handed.

The thought of screaming children deprived of holiday delights was interrupted by a yell from Paul as he manoeuvred the Jack Tar into the shallow waters. I turned to see him waving frantically, to get my attention. "Dave, Dave! Mayday!"

"Come on, Whizz!" I shouted needlessly; Whizz was already on the case. We ran towards the boat, where fellow volunteers Steph and Tug helped me load my rescue hero aboard, and I leapt into the puttering craft behind him. Tug, a fully-fledged member of the rescue team, was a muscly, strong man, a great asset to the cause. I never did remember him being called anything else – and in retrospect, I think it could have been because he could probably tow a vessel into harbor armed only with a fraying rope and a packet of Fisherman's Friends.

There was no time to lose; within seconds, Keith had spun the boat around and set us hurtling across the waves out of Rhossili Bay. "Reports of a dinghy drifting off Oxwich," he explained as we bounced along. "May have kids on board."

I sucked in my breath; dinghies were bad news. If there were any children onboard, or even adults, they would be in grave danger.

Keith picked up the VHF radio. "Mayday. Swansea Coastguard. This is the Jack Tar. Crew on board. Making good speed to Oxwich. Estimated on scene 14.05. Over."

Oxwich Bay is only six miles east of Rhossili Beach as the crow flies, but in summer holiday traffic, it can easily take half an hour or more by car. In the Jack Tar, we could do it in fifteen minutes, though we'd have to round three headlands and cover ten miles. Fifteen minutes can be a long time when there are people in trouble; speed and, of course, safety were utmost on our minds.

As Keith put the twin engine on full throttle, we zipped up our wetsuits and tried not to think of terrified children clinging to a lone dinghy in the open sea. These inflatables should be banned from the seaside; there's no way else to put it – they are a 'bloody nightmare'.

Although Oxwich is a calm, safe beach ninety-nine times out of a hundred, it is still the sea, and, like anywhere else, the sea is a moveable feast that can turn against you. You've got waves coming in; tides going in and out. You've got winds that can hit you sideways or blow you offshore. You can get dragged in a little whirlpool or find yourself in a 'rip' – one of the strong localised currents that move away from the shore.

People do not realize the ocean dangers or the influence of other boats and jet skis, which can chop up the water and make it move in unpredictable ways. The Bristol Channel has the second highest rise and fall of any tide in the world; that water can shift. Even on a beautiful sunny day like that Sunday afternoon in August 2008, the sea can move frighteningly quickly and catch coastal visitors unawares.

Steph was the first to spot the inflatable. It was a good quarter of a mile offshore, far enough out that the bathers on

Oxwich beach were mere pinpricks in the distance. As trained, Steph kept her arm extended in the direction of the dinghy so that Keith could make good speed to the right spot. The sky had turned darker suddenly, and an offshore wind had picked up. Conditions in the Bristol Channel around Swansea can change rapidly, as the Atlantic Ocean has few obstacles in its way to temper its forces... The situation was becoming more dangerous by the minute.

"Looks like two kids in there," said Tug, who was looking through binoculars.

"They got lifejackets on?" asked Keith.

"Don't think so," muttered Tug, but this was never time for chastisement.

We had to proceed more steadily now, or the wash from the boat's engine could tip the occupants into the water. Once we were within thirty meters, we could see two young girls, around primary school age, clinging onto the sides of the dinghy with all their might. They were clearly in deep distress.

Just then, a wave smashed the dinghy and flipped it over. The girls were tossed into the sea like brittle twigs, chased on an autumn day, and forced brutally from the anchors of their tree house. With no hesitation and not a glance at Whizz, or anyone else, I just jumped.

A moment later, there was a deluge of ocean spray as Whizz landed by my side – no need for instructions; he knew his job! We were close enough; one hundred, or possibly one hundred and fifty, yards from the girls. Their position was life-threatening; they had already drifted apart from the upturned dinghy and one another; they were each struggling on their own. They must have undoubtedly been distraught. I do not know if they were screaming or crying. I do not remember any emotion; not theirs, not mine. It's true what they say; the training kicks in.

I could not reach them both, but I managed to grab the youngest, a girl of eight or nine. Holding her securely and keeping her chin above water, I tried to calm her hysteria and assured her, "It's okay. You're okay!"

From what I could see, the other girl looked older. Her long, dark, dripping hair whipped across her face as she flayed in the ocean, desperately trying to keep afloat.

"Whizz! Go-oo!" I shouted. She was some twenty feet away by now and being carried further out to sea, but the current was no match for my strong Whizz. Within moments he was there.

"Hold!" I yelled as he swam close enough for her to reach out and grab him.

Goodness knows what this young schoolgirl thought when she saw Whizz's great sleek black head approaching on the waves... Was it some sea monster to finish her off? She was too far away now for me to provide much reassurance, so I kept it loud and simple. "DON'T BE AFRAID – GRAB HIS HARNESS, AND HE'LL DO THE REST!"

The girl stretched out her arm, but her fingers just missed the ring on Whizz's harness. She cried out in panic, and for a heart-split moment, I thought she had gone under. Whizz was never to give up; he circled and returned; moments later, there she was, her hand clearly gripping the ring, spluttering, but her head above water.

Splashing the surface of the water, as I had done hundreds of times in drills, Whizz swam back to me, pulling the girl behind him. 'Yes! Come on boy', I thought, mentally willing him on, though I didn't say anything out loud. Although Whizz was perfectly capable, rescue dogs need clear, concise instructions. Sometimes in drills, people get excited and say 'good boy' and 'well done' and all that, but that isn't what dogs want to hear at that moment. Clear and simple is the key.

As Whizz's hulking frame came within reach, I told the younger girl to grab hold of the ring on the other side of his harness, which she did until her knuckles were white. Then I gave Whizz one final instruction: "Boat!" He turned in the water and towed both the girls back to the Jack Tar while I swam alongside.

Tug and Steph had no problem lifting the girls out of the waves. The pair of them together weighed less than Whizz. Obviously, it took more effort to hoist one wet twelve-stone Newfie over the side, but at last, Whizz was onboard. Me? Well, I am always last, I suppose – and quite rightly so, victims and doggy heroes first. Finally, it was my turn to be dragged over the inflated tubes onto the deck of the boat, where I lay for a moment catching my breath.

Keith radioed the coastguard. "We've recovered the casualties. Two young girls. They seem well and not injured. We're taking them back to Oxwich beach now. Over."

The girls were shivering with cold and shock. Steph wrapped them in silver foil blankets and offered them a cup of tea from the flask in her backpack.

The youngest, a slip of a nine-year-old with short reddish hair, quickly calmed down once she saw she was safe, but the older child was wracked with tears. I knew then that they were sisters, and she felt responsible for her younger sibling, poor kid.

Barefoot and dressed only in swimming costumes, they had an extremely lucky escape, it was true. Now was not the time to scold them or give them a lecture on water safety. It was a time to lift their spirits and relieve their anxiety, keeping the conversation light as the Jack Tar carried us back to shore, towing the inflatable dinghy behind us.

"This is Whizz," I said. "Ever met a big dog like him before?" The girls looked at the black and white giant seated beside them with shy admiration and shook their heads. At that moment, as is his usual practice on completion of a mighty task, my dog decided to shake all the seawater from his thick coat.

"Eugh!" was the exclamation all around as we shared a proper soaking. Whizz didn't seem fussed, and it brought a smile to the girls' faces.

"You cuddle up to him if you want. He won't hurt you." I grinned.

The eldest reached out, still shuddering with sobs, and placed her hand on Whizz's back. He turned his humongous hairy face to hers, making her squeal and look away, but her cries came out as a giggle. The younger one laughed too, as she tried to pat the enormous saviour while dodging his big wet nose. Once Whizz had said hello, he turned his gaze back to his beloved view of the sea, and the girls were able to cuddle up. You could see them calming down and starting to breathe normally again.

"You're all right now," said Steph. "You're all right."

A crowd had gathered on the beach, and as we got closer, it was easy to spot the girls' mother, who was striding through the shallows to meet us, closely followed by another lady, who turned out to be her friend. Tears streamed down their faces as they helped to lift the girls out of the boat and hugged them for dear life."

"Isla! Rhona! Oh! Thank God, thank God!" cried their mother, covering them in kisses. "My girls!"

Keith took the children's details – Isla was eleven, Rhona was nine, and they were on holiday from Paisley in Scotland. He radioed the coastguard to say they had been reunited with their mum Claire. The girls appeared none the worse for their ordeal apart from more than a little humbleness and two pairs of blue lips. Locals brought hot chocolate and blankets to comfort the siblings, and a pair of paramedics arrived to check them over.

Pointing out Whizz to Claire, Keith explained how "That big dog over there" had saved the girls' lives.

"Thank you," she gulped, her voice cracking with gratefulness and emotion.

I could see her head was swimming with a mixture of relief, grief, joy, dread, and guilt. There was nothing I could do to make it better, so I just put a gentle arm around her shoulder and said: "Please don't worry; they'll be all right."

As for Whizz, his paws didn't even touch dry land; he stayed on the boat. As soon as Isla, Rhona, Claire, and Claire's friend Rachel were escorted away by the paramedics, we returned to the boat and found him sitting there with Tug, looking out to sea as if he couldn't wait to be off again.

"What took you so long, Dave?" he seemed to say as we hopped aboard, and Keith steered us out into the bay. "I've been sat here like a nagged walrus - Come on! Let's go swimming!'

"Well done, Whizzy," I said, giving his hairy head a ruffle.

Putting his paws up on the foredeck, he gained a better view of the sea. 'Well done for what, Dave?'

That was Whizz through and through. It was just another great day out at the seaside for him. He did not need my praise or my reassurance, or even my presence. A supremely confident dog, he just wanted to be out there feeling the wind in his fur and leaping into the Atlantic like his ancestors did hundreds of years ago.

For the rest of the afternoon, we stayed on the water, repeating rescue drills, with no more real-life mayday calls. Later, with Jack Tar safely moored at Swansea marina, Whizz padded ashore at last and let me shower the salty water off his coat, shaking half of it over me again, of course.

Keith wrote up the day's events in the logbook, stating that Whizz was a true hero who had excelled in his role as Great Britain's only canine lifeguard. Without him, I honestly doubted we could have saved both of those girls. It all finally began to sink in that night when we arrived back at my Auntie Mary's and gobbled up a hearty home-cooked meal.

"Well then, what have you boys been up to today?" she asked as we ravenously tackled steak and kidney with potatoes. "You've certainly both worked up an appetite."

Whizz's meal lasted seconds. He licked his bowl clean and settled down on the cool flagstones by Auntie Mary's hearth.

"It's been quite a day," I sighed.

It would be wrong to say that was the happy ending to the story. It took years for Isla and Rhona to get over the trauma, and Claire is still haunted by the events of that fateful day on the Gower Peninsula.

Like most mums, she was used to being pestered for things by her kids, but every day of that holiday, on the way to the beach, the girls had pleaded with her to buy them a blow-up dinghy. Every morning she had said 'no' – that is, until the morning before they were due to return home to Scotland. That morning she cracked.

Isla and Rhona were thrilled, and at first, all went well. The girls were ordered to stay in the shallows and not to splash anyone, and Claire stood at the edge of the water, watching them like a hawk. All seemed fine, and the girls were taking heed of the instructions and warnings.

After lunch, Claire and her friend Rachel stayed behind on the picnic blanket, devouring a punnet of fresh strawberries and reliving their teenage years by scoring 'hot male beach bums' marks out of ten. It was a well-earned diversion from their busy lives, but as they giggled, they did not notice people gathering at the edge of the sea.

Claire says she felt sick when she became aware of the crowd. She sprang to her feet and scoured the sea for the girls but could not see them or the dinghy anywhere. Her heart was racing, but time stood still, the voices around her muffled.

One cut through the fog – "They've been swept right out!" it said.

In the distance, she could just make out the flimsy inflatable with Isla and Rhona on board. When the dinghy capsized, her legs buckled beneath her, and she collapsed onto the wet sand.

"My heart felt like it had been ripped out," Claire told me later. "I screamed the most painful screech that still resonates within me. I felt completely helpless; all I could do was shout the same thing over and over. 'The girls can't swim! The girls can't swim!'"

If we had given Claire a hard time that day, it would have been nothing compared to the mental torture she heaped on herself. It's a parent's lot in life to get things wrong sometimes and to feel guilt. Whether the mistake changes your life or not is a bit of a lottery. There by the grace of God, and all that.

The months and years that followed were challenging for the family. Claire says Isla was petrified of water and would not venture away from her. Rhona suffered horrendous nightmares, and Claire herself lost confidence as a mother.

However, slowly and surely, they worked through the trauma and turned their lives around. The girls started one-to-one swimming lessons and occasionally even went to the beach. They also welcomed a dog into their family.

"We've named him Pugh after you," Claire told me. "With him by their side, the girls always feel safe." I felt choked with emotion.

Many years after that dreadful day, one morning in 2019, an envelope dropped on the mat. Inside was a letter wrapped in a white embossed card – it was from Claire. She told me that Isla was twenty-three and working as a flight attendant. Rhona was twenty-one and studying at St-Andrews University. The card was an invitation to Isla's wedding to be held near Paisley and the family's home.

Whizz is long gone, bless him, but I was asked to bring my dog Tizz, Whizz's cousin, to watch Isla walk down the aisle. What an honor that was, and what a wonderful day.

I am going to leave that as the 'happy-ever-after' moment for Isla, Rhona, and Claire, though I am sure, thanks to Whizz, they have many more exciting chapters to come.

Whizz to the rescue at Oxwich Bay

Chapter Nineteen: The Hoff – Baywatch

Whizz meets the iconic *Baywatch* lifeguard David Hasselhoff from the TV series!

The 'Hoff' was playing the evil Captain Hook character in Peter Pan at the Bristol Hippodrome. I remembered reading some literature sent to me by a German friend, that David once owned a black Newfoundland back in his native California. What a fabulous thing it would be for him to promote our charity in some way!

A trustee of our charity found out where David was staying and 'in for a penny, in for a pound' – I wrote a letter and handed it into the reception at the apartments situated in the centre of Bristol. A few days later, I was pleasantly surprised to receive a phone call from a man with a very distinct American accent... not actually 'The Hoff' himself, but his agent informing me that David would be delighted to meet Whizz and the rest of the dogs and would particularly like to converse with a young member of our team – who we shall call Tim.

A day and a time were arranged between performances when Whizz, the famous lifeguard, could meet his pretend counterpart. You could say both were heroes in their own way, but there the similarity ended.

'Mitch Buchannon' David Hasselhoff's Adonis *Baywatch* character, entertained millions of TV viewers, strutting his 'stuff' up and down the beach, surrounded by beautiful women almost dressed in bright red swimsuits. The emphasis was certainly on body tone in both sexes. The actual rescues, for most of the audience, were purely incidental.

Whizz, on the other hand, was not at all attracted to fair mermaids, or any human muscly form for that matter. Content with his own hairy body and bushy tail, all that interested our canine friend was water and rescuing bodies of any shape or form that were in trouble. Unlike 'Mitch', Whizz was completely unaware of the numerous glamourous groupies that followed his performances. The likes of Blue Peter presenter and former Miss Ireland Zoe Simon; American super-model Caprice Bourret; Carol Vorderman; and Sky TV presenter Freya Berry were amongst Whizz-fan-beauties.

I think Freya was the most memorable, though I doubt Whizz really noticed when he was challenged to rescue her as part of the TV coverage at the National Dragon Boat Festival at Bewl reservoir near Tunbridge Wells, Kent.

I do not think she was really impressed with the wet suit we gave her; it did not actually fit over her black thigh boots and only just squashed over her minute swimsuit. Not wishing to dash her image in the least, she promptly donned the boots on top of the wetsuit and thrust her phone into her cleavage on the unzipped upper part of the protective clothing. We let the phone go – not a safety issue, only financial when it would be destroyed by briny liquid, but the boots had to go.

To be fair, Freya dived superbly, and Whizz followed on with the rescue with his usual expertise. It turned out to be quite an amusing day in more ways than one, but a huge amount of money was raised for charity, and that was the whole objective of the event.

I was so pleased that David was going to meet Tim. Our young friend has a special place in all our hearts, and I will take a little time to tell his story.

Members of our charity foster children on a regular basis, and subject to all the usual safeguarding and medical checks, they were always made welcome within our team, and of course, they all adored Whizz. Tim was one of those needy children, along with a young man named Christopher.

Christopher had been in foster care for the best part of his life, and we all grew to love him dearly. The foster care authorities actually gave permission for Christopher to feature on the TV program; *'Extra Ordinary Dogs'*, with

Whizz. It was all filmed and posted on YouTube under the category of 'dogs of distinction'. Christopher is so proud of his stardom and makes sure everyone he comes across has a viewing or two.

Tim, also in foster care, was only five years of age and diagnosed with leukaemia. His biological parents were in denial of this very serious condition, and Tim was placed with Claire and Andrew, team members who often took children in with medical needs. This was a last-resort action on the part of the authorities and one which is never taken lightly.

Tim was not receiving any treatment for his leukaemia. His father was a qualified accountant, and his mother a school teacher; two intelligent, professional people, or so you would have thought. No one could really comprehend how you could let a five-year-old child suffer so much, and had the intervention not been made; death would be just around the corner. This poor young chap must have wondered what his life was all about.

Claire spent many nights and days with Tim Bristol Children's Hospital oncology ward. The journey was long and arduous and lasted a number of years. It was thanks to the dedication of the medical profession and the love and support of Andrew and Claire that Tim triumphed over this evil cancer and received the news we were all praying for - he had won the battle!

Some people comment on Tim's story, telling me that children are resilient and forget; I say otherwise. I remember my fantastic childhood, my wonderful parents, and many brilliant school friends. You never forget poignant things in your life, and Tim will never forget his war but will be greatly cushioned by the love, care, and affection Claire gave him.

Newfoundland friends decided to start a fund-raising project – in honor of the true life-saving care that our friend Tim had received at Bristol oncology. The appeal, aptly named 'Tim's Appeal', was fronted by a sponsored Newfoundland dog rescue day. All our dogs performed impeccably, and a massive £10,000 was raised.

Tim presented the cheque to the consultant who had helped rescue our proud survivor. With a huge grin spread across his face, I am sure he did not mind a few ruffles of his full head of hair.

We all felt Tim had gone through so much that he deserved a little treat. Claire and Andrew told me of Tim's love of football and that his real father supported Fulham FC. Tim's parents came from London, and that got my mind thinking.

We sent an email to Fulham football club and told them of Tim's battle with leukaemia and that he would love to watch them play. Fulham were keen to help and contacted us within the day, sending an invitation to attend a match on New Year's Day. The match was an all-London derby against West Ham United.

Neither Claire nor Andrew liked football and asked if I would take Tim to the match. Claire, pleased at the opportunity to shop to her heart's content in the January sales, was happy to drive us to the big city. We parked on the outskirts of the city and travelled together on the tube to Hammersmith.

Claire, armed with a big bag and a small credit card, shot off for some retail therapy, and I was left in charge of Tim. Not being his registered carer made me slightly anxious, though I knew he would be as safe as houses with me.

After a fair walk, we arrived at the ticket office, as per instructions, thinking we were just going to be given a pair of gems to watch the match. In fact, there was much more in store. Tim's eyes lit up as he was handed a Fulham shirt, along with a hoard of other small souvenirs bursting the seams of a carrier bag.

Following this presentation of gifts, a very pleasant gentleman gave us a tour of the ground and changing rooms.

The tickets were top notch, and we were taken to a hospitality box, complete with a steward, a set meal, and even our own private toilets – an absolute blessing when you are in charge of a young boy.

The icing on the cake? Fulham won the match – what an amazing day it was.

Tim continued to remain healthy, and we were ecstatic to see him well and back on his feet; both Claire and I felt we had really helped him along his path to recovery.

It was, therefore, a bitter blow to us all that the fostering authorities decided that Tim should go back and live with his mother. Despite our protests, it was to be, and thankfully, he continued to thrive and gained a scholarship to Bristol Cathedral School. His mother is now living a long distance away from us and made her home with another lady. Unfortunately, we did not see Tim after the reunite until Whizz was given the Animal Hero Award by the Daily Mirror.

Whizz was pretty poorly at that time and unable to travel to London to accept the award. Tim and Whizz had a superb bond, and I know Whizz would have been proud of his friend for accepting the award on his behalf.

It would also be a great opportunity for Claire to spend some time with Tim. Thankfully, through a third party, we were able to gain Tim's mother's agreement, and we picked him up from his home and travelled to London by train.

A fully paid-for trip, funded by the Mirror, there seemed no expense was spared, and we arrived at a prestigious hotel, having been booked two private rooms; one single for myself and another for Claire and Tim.

The ceremony was to be held at the posh Northumberland Hotel, and at 7 pm, precisely the limousines arrived to take us to the event. We were greeted by impeccably dressed ushers and directed to our reserved table.

Looking around at the splendour, I thought Tim might be a little overawed at the sea of celebrities scattered around the room. Accompanying him to the stage and to be greeted by Amanda Holden, Tim's broad smile told me otherwise. His grin lit up the whole place as the applause resounded around the room. It was an evening we would never forget, and the delight on Tim's face was priceless. The wonderful time in London was finished with a short sightseeing venture, as our train was not until later the following day – it was a tired but elated trio that arrived home that night.

Tim deserved all the treats that we could muster, and the day arrived when he would meet David Hasselhoff at the Bristol Hippodrome. The time was set for 'The Hoff' and his agent to greet us between performances. At the time, David had recently become engaged to a young Welsh lady, who was staying with him in the posh apartments opposite the theatre. It was not yet public knowledge, and our photographer, Martin, was hoping to take a photograph of them both. It would be a great opportunity to make some good money for the appeal.

Of course, Whizz was not to be left out and commanded much attention as Claire, Tim, and I waited outside the Hippodrome until the matinee audience had dispersed. Martin arrived carrying his camera equipment, and we were directed to a large room on the upper floor overlooking Bristol city centre.

Hayley, a little reserved, kept her distance, but it was the tall, handsome 'Hoff', face still smudged with stage makeup, that strode across the room straight to Whizz, throwing his arms around to give him a big hug. The affinity he had with dogs was evident in abundance.

Martin was able to secure fabulous shots of Whizz and the Hoff, some posed but most natural. We told the story of Tim's long battle with leukaemia and the fundraiser, 'Tim's Appeal'. David needed no encouragement; he was very happy to do all he could to help. More photos of Whizz, Tim, and The Hoff were taken, and although a snap of Hayley and

David was not forthcoming, the whole meeting was a massive success.

David donated autographed souvenirs, including his *Baywatch* Torpedo – the red-shaped rescue piece of equipment used in the show and also signed his name across a photograph of Whizz in action at Oxwich Bay, adding the words, 'The real Baywatch Star'.

There are a few stories circulating around about David. I can honestly say I found him a most pleasant and accommodating person who was prepared to put himself out to help others. He and Hayley visited oncology the next day, greeting each child in turn and showering them with gifts. The care team were just as excited to meet them, and it was a fantastic gesture for David and Hayley to make.

Tim loved the experience of it all... I am not sure about Whizz; I think was a little bewildered being smothered by a large American icon – until he spied the red torpedo... 'Ah... a rescue man... he must be a cool kind of guy!'

Whizz meets up the Baywatch star David Hasselhoff

Chapter Twenty: The Beginning of the Last Goodbye

Today I closed the door to the past and opened a new chapter to the future. All good things must come to an end, and sadly nothing lasts forever.

Following a training session at Oxwich Bay on the Gower Peninsula, I noticed that Whizz had a small abrasion to his front right paw. Little did I know at the time that this was the start of his gradual demise.

The cut became visible as I was washing Whizz with fresh, clean water; the usual practice after swimming. The water turned slightly pink as the bleeding presented itself, but after the dousing and a good clean-up, it did not look too serious. Daily bathing the wound in salt water normally heals these minor cuts in a few days; I had no worries about continuing our normal walking routine.

After ten days of regular treatment, the injury did not seem to be healing as I had hoped, so I decided a precautionary trip to the vet would be advisable.

Whizz was familiar with surgery visits and would be happy to toddle along to any kind of vet. I, however, not so. The horrific experience with leptospirosis lay heavily on my mind, and I was extremely reluctant to re-visit the practice with whom I had encountered so many difficulties. Whizz was very near to death, and the delay in identifying the problem and administering the correct treatment could have quite easily sealed his fate. I was unhappy about the whole affair, and I knew it was only Whizz's strength and determination that pulled him through that difficult time.

I had no idea, at first, which practice to use. My trust had been severely damaged. Then, I remembered Maisie, a brown bitch of around four years of age whose owner had fallen on hard times. Due to a marriage breakdown, a mother, two children, and a massive Newfoundland found themselves in temporary accommodation and in financial difficulty. Maisie had been loved, but the ongoing treatment had left her owner with a huge vet's bill, which she could not afford to pay, and certainly, the further veterinary care she needed was going to be impossible to fund.

It was with great sadness that there was no choice but for Maisie to be rehomed and the Newfoundland Club of the UK stepped in to help. They offered to pay for the bills incurred to date if Maisie was found a more suitable environment to live in. My services, together with Debbie, a team associate and longstanding member of the charity, were engaged by the club to carry out the somber task of collecting Maisie from her family.

It was not a job I would place on anyone's shoulders, but Maisie's welfare had to come first. Thankfully the children were at school when we made our way to Weston-Super-Mare, and having obtained the required signatures on the paperwork, Maisie was taken from her tearful owner and placed into my van.

Debbie had agreed to take Maisie under her wing at her home, at least for the time being, but she did not look at all well, and it was obvious she needed urgent care. It was therefore decided that we would take Maisie to Rowes veterinary group, North Bristol, a practice that Debbie had used for a number of years and had given glowing reports. After explaining the situation to them, Maisie was welcomed, immediately taken in, assessed, and kept overnight. Debbie collected her the following day and ensured that during the next few weeks, her new companion attended all the necessary appointments and endured the extended treatment that enabled her to make a full recovery.

It was kind of Debbie to take on Maisie; I am not sure how Whizz and Ted would have reacted to a new housemate – and a lady at that. It was bad enough, with the pair of them lunging at me with full force as if I had been away for days when I returned home that day. It was perfectly obvious they smelt the tantalising aroma of the fair sex as I unlocked the

Fort Knox five-bar gate. I wondered whether to face imminent suffocation or leg it off into the woods and dive into a stream!

As regards to the payment, I contacted the practice with a personal offer to settle the bill, but the senior partner of the practice was more than happy to carry on with the treatment without the need for upfront remuneration and was prepared to wait for as long as it took for the Newfoundland club to sort it out. I was very grateful to Mr. Rowe for this gesture; his heart was certainly with Maisie and her plight.

After a month or so, Maisie found her forever home with an elderly lady named Mrs. Whyte. She lived in the middle of nowhere on a small holding situated on the borders of Oxfordshire and Berkshire. Having recently lost her previous Newfoundland, it was a perfect solution for both of them. The companionship was to go on for seven long fantastic years, with Maisie rarely leaving the old lady's side, contrary to her other dog Dylan, a rascal of a terrier who was forever absconding and getting up to all sorts of mischief.

It was to our amusement, as we arrived to deliver Maisie to her wonderful new surroundings that were greeted by the offending Houdini. Dylan, infinitely excited at the prospect of a new sister, promptly bounded towards us with perfect adeptness, considering he was burdened with an extremely large cardboard sign tied around his neck, clearly displaying his telephone number in huge black lettering.

It was as good an ending as it could be to a sad story. Mrs. Whyte kept in touch, and always a festive card blessed our mantlepiece each Christmas. It was always signed by Mrs. White from herself, Maisie, and Dylan; at least the wild terrier still returned now and again to his base and had not packed his bags and gone to London to seek his fortune.

I will never forget the kindness and understanding of Mr. Rowe. There was, therefore, no contest; this was the vet I would trust with Whizz.

My first visit to Rowes veterinary practice with Whizz was just as a precaution. I wanted to make sure that his foot with heal and that all would be well. I made an appointment for an early morning visit with Whizz.

As we drove up the M5 motorway in my van, I had no idea that we were to undertake this short journey many times in the future. After all, it was a minor injury, and I was not really worried. Indeed, when we parked up in the large car park, Whizz leapt out of the van as if he was off to a party. I had a mind that we would be in and out with a handful of antibiotics, and that was that.

The facilities were great; all mod cons, with its own twenty-four-hour hospital on site. We waited our turn and sat in a pleasant room. I say sat, but you know Whizz by now. He was not a jot bothered by his injury and was more interested in the fuss he was receiving from all the clients and the staff.

Eventually, we trotted into a consultation room to be faced by a very young vet, who was minute compared to the huge form of the patient that patiently stood by my side. I could see that she was more than a little apprehensive as we both concluded there was no way we were going to be able to fit, never mind lift Whizz onto the examination table.

It took a little explanation that Whizz would do no more than lick her to death to reassure her that she was quite safe and she would not need a muzzle or a strait jacket to carry out the examination. In fact, I could almost see her heart melt as Whizz held up his poorly digits for her to see.

It transpired she was new to the practice, and this was her first day. Making conversation, as you do, I found out the young lady was well qualified, having studied at Liverpool University and specialising in equine care. I knew the university was renowned for its excellence, particularly in horse expertise.

Maybe, this was why Rowes bestowed Whizz upon her; he was certainly as big as a horse. For her very first consultation, I did wonder if this was the reason that she had been propelled in at the deep end.

All the right questions were asked; how did it happen; how long had it been like this? Did Whizz seem out of sorts or different in any way? I answered with confidence; it was just a cut, nothing more, no pain; Whizz was his normal jolly excitable self.

I tried to ignore the pensive look on her face as she gave me the suspected diagnosis...This poor young lady had her first client of the day, and that first client had a suspected tumour. I was stopped dead in my tracks. Having lost my mother and dogs to cancer before, I could not believe this was the case with Whizz...My Whizz, who had battled leptospirosis and, against all odds, had triumphed in his conflict.

A senior vet, Liz, was summonsed, and I was so glad to hear that she did not think this was the case. As I had anticipated, Liz prescribed a course of antibiotics and told me to keep the wound clean and change the dressing twice a day. Whizz was to have regular check-ups to keep an eye on the healing process.

Whizz was brilliant with the dressings, making no attempt to chew them off; he just took it all in his stride. I was very grateful for this because I do not know how they would have found an Elizabethan collar big enough for his enormous neck. It surely would have been a case of a ruff the size of a concertinaed corrugated roof section, necessitating an extension of the saloon dog flap!

Much as I would have liked Whizz to swim in salty water to digest its healing properties, the vets were adamant that swimming was out of the question. The paw was taking its time to recover, with no apparent improvement, but on the other hand, it was not getting any worse. Whizz was gutted; his huge soppy eyes longing and pleading for a dip – how hard it was to say no, and he could not understand why.

News travelled the world that Whizz, the famous rescuer, was grounded and his swimming curtailed. What was to be done? A huge stroke of luck ensued; a close friend, Josse Latreille, employed by the Canadian police, came up with the remarkable idea of providing a waterproof shoe similar to those worn by their dogs to protect their paws in icy weather. The shoes had already been used successfully in the UK with the fire brigade - kitting out the dogs that scoured the charred remains of a blaze. So why not one for Whizz?

Measurements were taken, and photos were sent to Canada; I do not think a bigger dog shoe could have ever been manufactured before. It was a very excited Dave, and an even more inquisitive Whizz, that ripped open the parcel that arrived a few weeks later. Of course, Ted did not get a look in – no way was he going to get his teeth into this treasure.

We were amazed to find not one, but two shoes, firstly mistaking them for a pair, then realizing they had kindly sent a spare. They looked like the wet shoes we wore as humans- black with vibrant red markings, with similar Velcro straps to keep them secure, but obviously 'doggy shaped'.

"Right then, Whizz; you shall go to the ball!" I knelt like Prince Charming, sliding on the glass slipper. It was a perfect fit on my Cinders.

"Right then, Dave, I can stay up way past midnight – let's get cracking!"

As if Whizz was not a celebrity before, he was propelled further into the limelight as the media cottoned on to the story. We were bombarded with requests for photos, and the scoop of the 'Mountie rescue of the Newfie rescuer' were plastered all over the tabloids. Whizz was back in action and loving every minute of the return of the canine lifeguard of the beaches of Wales, ensuring the safety of swimmers and others in trouble on the sea.

Life was almost back to normal, changing his dressings twice a day and bathing his sore foot with salty water. Whizz continued with the antibiotics and was back to his happy self once again. The walks took a little longer, not because of injury, but the many questions fired at us both as onlookers surveyed the big dog with in his wellie. Liz continued to monitor Whizz's condition and became a close family friend as the weeks turned into months.

It was at the fourteenth-month stage that things began to take a turn for the worse; the wound was refusing to heal up and slowly increasing in size. It became obvious to all that this was no ordinary abrasion. Liz asked if I was happy for her to have Whizz in for the day to do a biopsy. Of course, I was not at all happy, but it had to be done – whatever the outcome, Whizz's health was all important, and if the correct treatment could be found, it would be.

Whizz was no trouble and his usual laid-back self. The biopsy was done, and I picked up my Newfie friend as soon as I had the phone call from Liz... Then the awful wait began.

Cancer seems to be the most common cause of death in both humans and pets. Today you almost hear of nothing else. I had lost Harry, Dylan, and Bear to the dreadful illness, and I did not want to lose Whizz as well.

Speculation as to the causes vary from year to year. Some think it is, maybe, due to the intensive feeding of dry dog food, then other theories arise – who knows. With the advancement in medicine, we are all living longer, and other ailments arise.

I swallowed deeply as I heard Liz's voice when I answered the call. The results were in, and they were inconclusive. I did not know whether this was good news or bad. The growth was still expanding, and after consultation with the senior practitioners, the decision was made to take another biopsy.

The results did not really come as a surprise. All the vets were of the same opinion, the tumour was cancer, and the only chance Whizz had of survival was to have an amputation of the leg.

My heart was broken; it was a situation beyond belief. Whizz would never be able to sustain his massive eighty-five kilos on three legs without major health implications. His days as 'Whizz', the life-saving Newfie, would be no longer. Whizz would not mentally cope with any of it. This was a dog that could jump from a boat at full speed. This was a dog that could pull twelve people at once, and above all, this was a dog that was strong and proud, and I knew the devastation of disablement would be too much for him to bear.

Whizz had come into my life through the back door. We had been separated for the first year of his life through circumstance and no fault of his own. I was not about to let him suffer and slide away lonely and depressed. I had to make the awful decision to let him go whilst we were still together and whilst he was still happy. It was one of the worst choices I have ever had to make; yet, really, there was no choice -no choice at all.

Liz had been with Whizz though-out his ordeal. They had shared many special moments together, and he was completely at ease in her presence. She was the only person I wanted and trusted to do the inevitable – we would say goodbye to my treasured Whizz together.

Liz was temporarily employed at Rowes Wotton-Under-Edge practice, covering annual leave. It was further away than our normal surgery, but that was fine with me - It had to be Liz. Arrangements were made for the fateful day, and I also contacted Animal Haven Crematorium, where two years previously, I had taken Bear. I found it so hard to believe it was that long ago, and now, another of my friends was to follow in his footsteps.

On a cold and frosty January morning, I called the boys and set off on our daily walk. I was determined to start the day with the normal routine, but how could it be? How could it possibly be my last walk with Whizz – I felt sick to the stomach.

Ted and Whizz were none the wiser; Ted charging ahead, whilst Whizz gazed at his insane brother with wide eyes and a sense of boring acceptance. "What a plonker, Dave!"

We walked, as we often did, through the fields and along the church path to Saint Michael's. The twelfth-century building stood quietly inviting, holding out a hand of comfort as I walked into the porch with Whizz at my side. It was the last occasion we would stand together, as we had many times before, but this time in deep reflection, seeking solace. I felt slightly numb, and it is hard to tell the story, even to this day, without tears trickling from my eyes.

I do not even recall Ted being with us inside this sacred place, as I used the time to recite the Lord's prayer and remember all the friends, animals, and humans that I have loved in my life. I guess he must have been foraging around the gravestones, looking for colourful blooms to decimate or sniffing out a lonely squirrel hiding in the undergrowth. Whatever he was doing, I knew he would not be far. This time was for Whizz, myself, and prayers together. I prayed for courage and strength; I prayed for God to be with me as I faced this day of inevitability with sadness, and I prayed for Whizz to find peace.

Hanging around, the house would only make things worse, so I returned Ted to Jean's capable hands and opened the van doors. I had carefully laid a comfortable blanket inside, but I do not think Whizz really noticed – in he jumped as usual, happy and bouncing around, excited to tackle the trials of the day... I always wondered if he knew... if he did, it was not apparent in any way, and I was determined to keep things normal, for as long, as possible.

Although it was around 7 am, the expected build-up of works traffic did not materialise on the M5 as I winged my way northwards, past Avonmouth docks, with its vast area of industrial structures and mounds of stacked up unsold cars, awaiting their forever homes. Past the reminders of our materialistic existence, the countryside emerges once again, and the beautiful Severn Estuary glistens as the morning sunrise lights up the murkiness of the night waters.

It was here I suddenly decided to halt our journey, even just for a little while. Veering off at junction eighteen, driving along the coastal road, and turning into the quiet village of Severn Beach, I parked the van. We had visited this little place many times before, taking walks along the promenade and taking in the sea air. Whizz could not wait to sniff the salty air, and his eyes lit up when I opened the doors and allowed him to leap onto the path.

On our final walk together – along the coastal path, I could scarcely take it all in. I watched Whizz shaking his head, lapping up the feel of the wind on his face, and breathing in his love of the sea. I wanted this to be my last memory of my beloved friend and tried not to think of the dreadful morning ahead.

Wotton-Under-Edge is a quaint small village, traditional with its limestone cottages and Victorian-looking shops. At first, it was difficult to find the vets, and I was disinclined to ask anyone. Eventually, after circuiting the town, I found the practice along a small country lane on the outskirts. The car park was eerily empty; I checked my watch.... approaching 9 am – nearly time.

I left Whizz in the van, his familiar place, his last familiar place. It would be so much easier and advisable to treat him there. Checking in at reception, I returned to my morbid grey vehicle and sat in the driver's seat, constantly fidgeting and looking in the mirror for Liz and her veterinary nurse. A crunch of the gravel invaded my ears; another glance in the mirror and the pair were walking towards us.

Not a word was spoken as I opened the side door of the van sliding it fully open with Whizz settled on the van's floor. I looked into his eyes, and for the very first time I can remember, he looked so sad. At that point, he knew. My Whizz, with senses and intuition beyond the comprehension of man, knew. My eyes began to water, and the tears rolled down my cheeks. He knew as the nurse shaved a small section on his front leg. He knew as Liz injected the drugs into the drip. His solemn eyes glistened as he gave me his final loving look – then he fell to the floor and was still. Silently, Liz placed the stethoscope of Whizz's lifeless body and gave me a nod before retiring to the surgery and leaving me to my grief.

How long I sat in the van trying to collect my thoughts and gain some kind of composure, I do not know, but I was suddenly aware of the time; we had to be at the crematorium at 10.30 that morning.

My eyes were still flooded, it was difficult to drive, and I had to stop to pull myself together. Onward, then through Westerleigh village and past the New Inn pub. Ironically, this was the place where Jean and myself purchased our first dog, Jade. Nostalgia reared its head in abundance as I thought of all my dogs and the happy times we had spent together.

Havens Rest was not far from Westerleigh crematorium, reserved for us humankind. At the end of a short narrow lane, the cottage and outbuildings stood slightly insignificantly compared to the large buildings adjacent to the grounds. My thoughts turned to Bear, and here we were again, this time with Whizz.

A very pleasant lady opened the cottage door and, pre-empting the size of my Newfie, informed me that she had engaged the help of two men to carry Whizz to the incinerator. They were supposed to tackle this task themselves; owners were not generally allowed near the furnace. However, I could not leave my Whizz; I had to be with him to the end.

Thus, it was, the three of us, carried Whizz, wrapped in his comfort blanket, across the yard, into the stiflingly hot building, and stood in front of the oven. The men opened the doors, and the heat blasted my face as we gently slid Whizz into the fire.

I stepped back and watched as the flames engulfed the most amazing and loving dog I had ever owned. There would never be another – My Whizz was gone.

Whizz as we remember him

Chapter Twenty-One: The Legacy

A few days after I said my last goodbye to Whizz, Animal Haven called me to ask if I wanted the ashes. I was still choked with emotion; the thought of returning to the crematorium filled me with dread. What was the point of keeping the ashes? Did I want a reminder of that dreadful day; the demise in the van, or the hot flames powering the raging furnace; the heat blasting my face as the door was opened to receive my Whizz?

Bear's ashes stood on the shelf in my garage for months; rarely did I look at them. Eventually, I gained permission to scatter them in the garden of remembrance at Little Bridge House Children's Hospice. To my mind, I prefer to think of my dogs with happy memories - memories of long walks in the countryside; running free with the wind blowing through ruffled fur; the delights in their demeanour as they succeeded in their rescue work; and the laughter of the children as they frolicked around their canine friends, cheering any somber mood. Most of all, I remember the companionship and bonds we all formed; more than just friendship – every one of them was family.

As for Whizz and myself, after a difficult start for us both, we were destined through fate to share our lives together, flourishing into wonderful times spent. No box of ashes could ever take the place of those memories, and nor should it. It was, therefore, for all these reasons I did not return to Animal Haven. Whizz was in my heart as 'my Whizz' would stay forever.

Friends of mine have experienced the loss of a loved dog; the pain is often too much for them to bear. Of course, it is tragic, but I look at things a little differently. It is better to have loved than never loved at all. If I had ever thought the bereavement of an animal would be too much to bear, I would have been blessed with one friend, one dog, and one companion.

Despite my philosophy, I was totally devastated by Whizz's death; I was not sure I would ever want another Newfie again. We still had Terrible Ted, but he had more of a bond with Jean – a lady's dog if ever there was one. It was a few weeks later I resolved to reset my mind and collect my thoughts, and I took myself away for a few days.

It was on my return to the cottage that I noticed Debbie's van parked outside. That in itself was not unusual, she had kindly made a daily visit to walk Ted, but this was early in the morning. The garden was quiet; no Ted came careering through the prize blooms to greet me. Strangely, the side door was shut tight. 'Oh, Lord,' I thought, 'what's Ted done now!'

What met my eyes could not have been further from the truth. Debbie sat with a gorgeous Landseer puppy on her lap and Jean with another black and white bundle of fluff in her arms. As soon as they saw me, they began to squirm. Placed on the floor, they were even more excited at the newcomer that had come to play and made a beeline for my trouser legs. All I can say is thank goodness they could not reach further than my knees, or it would have been another trip to A and E.

Not content with wrecking my clothes, they then decided to start on Ted – music to his ears. It was all getting a little out of hand; thus, the trio was ushered out into the garden to destroy what was left of the flowers.

Debbie had been to Monique's house in Dorset. This lady had originally bred Whizz before he ended up at Lucy's kennels. The puppies were brother and sister and as close to Whizz's genetics and breeding as you could ever get. Their mother had been taken to France to mate with a highly prized and renowned Newfoundland stud dog, as had Whizz's parent before.

'Would I take one...or two?' Oh dear, how could you resist!

The female was splendid, with markings near perfect to Whizz's colours. The boy, less so, but strong and healthy looking. Much as I could have succumbed to both, the obvious was the dog, as we have never had bitches in the past.

This pretty little lady was, after much thought, named Doris, and off she went to her forever home. Now what to call the dog? That was my choice, and I have always remembered my dad's favorite saying and those amusing words carved into his marble gravestone – 'There, Tizz.'

For those of you who are not familiar with the Bristolian language that nobody north of Swindon understands... this means – 'that's it.' The choice was made – there Tizz was, in all his glory, enveloped in cuteness overload.

Tizz grew very quickly, as Newfoundland puppies do; Ted had a partner in crime and a friend once again. Although Tizz was as strong as an Ox and tougher than any other Newfoundland I have owned, it turned out, as it does on occasions, he did not take to swimming at all. He was a loveable softie who much preferred to spend his time with his partner in crime. A replacement for Whizz there would never be, and as much as we tried with tasty titbits, Tizz would not even come close. To Tizz, the sea was some kind of scary monster, spitting froth at his paws every time he ventured near a wave – one drop of salty brine and he was off. I guess that's what makes our dogs individuals – you cannot make them do what they do not want to do... and why should we?

The animal charity PDSA awarded Whizz a Posthumous Order of Merit Medal for his outstanding courage and life-saving skills. It was sad that he did not live long enough to receive it in his body. Tizz took his place at the ceremony, held at the Isle of Dogs in London. I was incredibly proud that day, but with very mixed emotions. I would like to think he would have been watching as his 'little brother' wagged his tail with delight as the medal was placed around his neck.

I am a normal sort of guy with no thoughts about ghosts or spirits, but I do wonder sometimes. A week or so after my mother's funeral, there was an incident I would not forget. Working in my joinery shop, I heard a lady's voice and glanced into the concave mirror, strategically placed in order for me to see, well in advance, anyone approaching the shop floor. Many of the machines pose a dangerous risk to the public, and I was very conscious of safety. The middle-aged lady was not familiar to me but talked as she walked towards me. She told me things about my mother that only my mother knew, and that Mum was fine and I was not to worry about her.

The lady was not a customer, a salesperson, or did not even seem to be a fortune-teller, as has been known to grace my presence in the past. This was different; something I cannot explain, and it does make you question life and, indeed, your own sanity. Of course, I kept the experience to myself – my work colleagues would have either sent me home for being drunk on the job or called an ambulance to cart me away.

Three years after Whizz passed away, cheeky Ted also succumbed to cancer. Once again, I endured the dreadful day as Liz ended his last ride in my van. This time, Animal Haven refused to allow me to place Ted into the oven. Instead, he was laid in a small chapel of rest. Assurances from the lady owner of the crematorium that he looked at peace had little effect on me; like Whizz, he was no more.

Ted was mischievous, who, I am sure, tested Whizz's patience, as he did all of us, on numerous occasions. But he was a lovable rogue, and I would like to think he is there with Whizz, scampering around in the heaven they call Rainbow Bridge, creating havoc with young Christian from the children's hospice.

Sadly, my bereavement was not to stay only with Whizz and Ted. My beloved wife, Jean, passed away at the beginning of the COVID pandemic. Only a handful of people were allowed at the burial, which was particularly upsetting as Jean was an extremely religious lady and the treasurer of the local church. It was just myself, my brother and sister, the vicar, and, thankfully, Tizz. Jean had a particular bond with him, and it would have been so distressing if he had not been present.

A year later, Tizz was to follow in their footsteps. He had been plagued with an ongoing condition that caused his stomach to bloat. This particular bout was serious, and I knew Tizz was in trouble and rushed him to the vet.

Covid has affected us all in one way or another, and I understand restrictions are necessary; but it was very frustrating to be sat outside the practice, answering questions about finances and insurance – information they already had – when Tizz was in a life-or-death situation. Eventually, Tizz was taken into surgery to release the gas. Unfortunately, the treatment was unsuccessful, and I had an agonising conversation over the telephone, the tragic outcome of which was to let Tizz pass away peacefully.

As if I was not distraught enough with the loss of Jean, I now found myself, for the first time in my life, without a dog. The cottage was eerie, quiet, and soulless. My normal early morning walk seemed pointless, yet somehow, I could not break that routine. Poo bags and leads, discarded in the kitchen, I set off across the fields towards the church to say my prayers, as I had done for the last forty years – this time, I was alone. My eyes fogged with tears as I blubbered out my thoughts and tried to finish my worship; I felt like all the world had been ripped from under my whole body.

My feet trudged through the dewy grass, and out of habit, I continually looked over my shoulder to see if the dogs were behind me, charging around and foraging amongst the undergrowth for hidden treasures. The trail was silent, save for the tweet of birds enjoying the sun rising to light up the sky above. It was then I saw it. The most colourful, beautiful stunning rainbow I had ever seen. Gleaming and vibrant, I shaded my eyes whilst I stared in awe at the perfect arc.

Was this a sign that Tizz had travelled over Rainbow bridge? Call me what you like, a 'nutter', a spiritualist, or whatever; I am convinced it was, and the big softy is sitting cuddling up to Jean.

No miracle visions had ever appeared after Whizz passed over. It is my belief that he is still within me, and that will never change. We are inseparable, and death is not going to change that one iota.

I have been lucky enough to share my life with several dogs, each one with a character of its own, and each one loved unconditionally. As with humans, they are all different, and it would be a sad world we live in if they were not. But Whizz, he was special, and I treasure the times we experienced together with mixed emotions, recalling the good and bad things that emerged as we travelled along the path we shared.

Whizz evolved from a scared puppy, caged and ignored for the first year of his life, into a dog who was a faithful companion, friend, and ultimate lifesaver, the likes of which I will never see again.

This book has been a long time in the making, and it is my humble legacy dedicated to a dog who was one in a million, a dog who strode from 'Zero to Hero'.

Tim Animal Hero Awards to receive Whizz's award

Epilogue

When I was asked to co-write a book about a dog, I must admit I was slightly apprehensive. Far from my normal genre of black comedy, family life, and hints of mystery, I did wonder, quite frankly, if I was 'up to the job'.

How could one compete with the likes of Lassie, Snowy, and Greyfriars Bobby, and was there room in the market for another doggie masterpiece?

My fears were completely allayed as soon as I met David and heard his tale of Whizz and the amazing journey of the life they had travelled together. I knew from the outset that this story had to be told.

This story had to be told because Whizz was, without a doubt, a superhero of his day – saving the lives of many who, without our canine friend, would not place feet on terra firma today.

This story had to be told because Whizz enriched everyone with natural compassion to love and protect...and this story had to be told of the unbreakable bond between one man and his Newfie companion.

I did not have the privilege of knowing Whizz when he was alive. Thus I, and you, the reader, met this wonderful creature through words and pictures, perceiving the admiration and love that shines between the lines. I followed his development, progressing from a scared lump of fluff to the magnificent animal he grew to be. At times, it felt a little intrusive – who was I to speak of death and bereavement? Yet, it is part of the tale, and we conquer the sadness to allow Whizz to live on in our minds. Through laughter and tears, we came to know the friendships and dared to share in intimate emotions, erupting through a sea of heroic rescues.

I can truly say by the end of this book; Whizz had become a part of me. To have known him padding our earth would have been an honor, but also, it seems strangely irrelevant now. That, however, is the whole point of our writings; if you have been touched by the contents and feel the same, then our task is well done.

The whole world needs to know about Whizz – in that way, our one-in-a-million, zero-to-hero Newfie wonder will never fade away and receive the recognition and tribute he thoroughly deserves.

Other books available from this author:

Follow Marcia on her life journey in this hilarious, sentimental, and heart-warming series. You will surely be drawn into her world and untangle a few mysteries along the way!

Available on Amazon and to order in good bookshops, these novels have achieved five-star reviews.

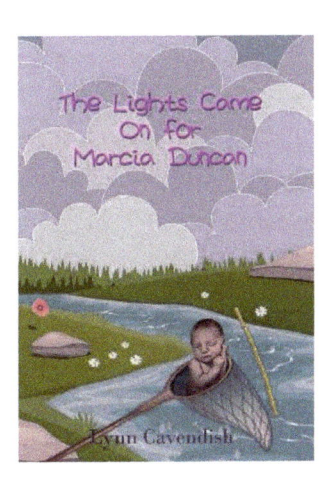

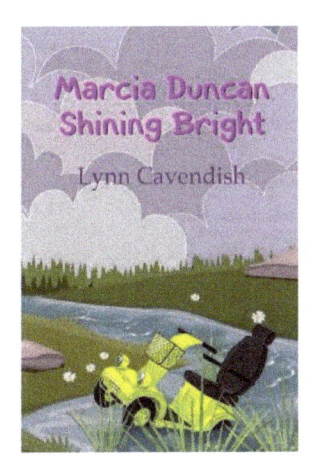

Lightning Source UK Ltd.
Milton Keynes UK
UKHW020958111122
411963UK00011B/49

9 781915 662750